HEALING WHISPERS
FROM
SPIRIT
GUIDES

Bridging the Gap Between
Life and the Afterlife with
a Death Doula's Wisdom

BY
HELEN GRETCHEN JONES

ISBN Paperback: # 979-8-9904373-0-2
ISBN Electronic: # 979-8-9904373-1-9
Library of Congress Control Number: # 2024909379

Publishing Consultant: PRESStinely, PRESStinely.com

Portions of this book are works of nonfiction. Certain names and identifying characteristics have been changed.

Printed in the United States of America.

Helen Gretchen Jones

HelenGretchenJones.com

Disclaimer

The author's intent is only to offer information of a general nature to help you in your quest for emotional, physical, and spiritual well-being. In the event you use any of the information in this book for yourself, the author and the publisher assume no responsibility for your actions. This publication is not intended as a substitute for the advice of a healthcare professional.

This book is dedicated to:

Taylor, Ty, and Elle

TABLE OF CONTENTS

Introduction

I awoke one June morning to a Voice telling me I would write a book.

"Write a book?" I asked.

"Yes. It will cover a lot of information and will take you just two years to complete."

"What should I write about?"

"Write what you know."

Throughout my life's journey, this Voice has never steered me wrong, but this news surprised me. Where would I even begin? The thought of it was overwhelming. *Surely there are people more qualified than me,* I thought. I did a quick outline. I settled on jotting down the only thing I could be sure of—my personal experiences as a Death Doula.

As a Death Doula, I accompany my clients holistically through the process of dying. I am blessed to have witnessed many extraordinary people on their end-of-life journey—and some of my most transformative moments have been spiritual events at the deathbeds of my clients. To respect the privacy of these individuals, I have changed their names and the circumstances of their journeys, but in no way have these alterations changed the integrity of their experiences or lessons.

While deathbed transitions to the Spirit world are always profound, the subtle "otherworldly" events that happen in our environment can be just as life changing. Communication from Spirit (and even from my Higher Self) has placed me in a serendipitous, unique position to help others find meaning and purpose in their lives. So, I am also a Life Doula. Each love-filled experience I have at a patient's bedside leaves me feeling inspired, content, and grateful.

Everyone has a voice, a story to tell. Through our stories, we can express the Self authentically, strengthen our ability to see ourselves in others, and (hopefully) discover a sense of inspiration and fearlessness on our life's journey. All my clients have amazing stories, and I am honored to share some of their experiences in this book. I hope their courageous accounts will help you learn that each of us can connect to something greater than our physical selves.

The Voice taught me to connect with the mystical world at an early age. Connecting to something greater than ourselves—God, the Universe, Source, All That Is, Oneness, our Higher Self or whatever vocabulary we find best suited for us—is called mysticism. Having a mystical experience means connecting to the Higher Power within us and allowing that wisdom to shape our lives. Ever since I can remember, I have been able to perceive mystical energies around me and tap into my surroundings with heightened insight.

When I was a child, the Voice was a comforting reminder to me that everything was okay, even when I felt unsure. When I felt insecure, I retreated to the bathroom, sat in an empty bathtub, and meditated. No one in my family practiced meditation, so I was not aware of what I was doing, but I would sit or lie down, take deep breaths, and focus on the silence, allowing my thoughts to dissipate. Sometimes the Voice would find me during these moments of peace, sometimes not.

The Voice has always been a reassuring, positive guide in my life's ups and downs, lessons, and accomplishments. It does not just deliver helpful commentary, it has weight and a familiar, soothing presence. It sounds masculine sometimes and at other times feminine, but it always comes from somewhere close.

The Voice is not singular—it comes from a collective source. Sometimes I feel a hand resting on my shoulder or my back. At first, this startled me, but now it is comforting. The Voice comes when I am filled with self-doubt. When I'm trying to be brave and overcome fears, it inspires and encourages me. Although the Voice originates in my mind, I can differentiate its beautiful inspirations from my thoughts. Its impressions come quickly, like a download of information I sort and interpret at a slower rate.

Sometimes I see the Voice. At times, it looks like golden-white beams of light, and when I focus on them, a being takes shape. Or, the white light ripples into waves of many colors—seemingly solid and transparent at the same time. Sometimes, the Voice appears in radiant balls of blue light. I recognize the Voice—these beings of light—as Spirit.

Spirit is a collective consciousness, but with an awareness of individual personalities. One way of envisioning this is through a traditional Eastern analogy: Spirit is like the ocean. Each personality is like a wave, emerging from one great collective body, experiencing itself as a wave, and then returning to the sea, its Source. Within this ocean of experiences, personalities live and contribute to the prevailing wisdom and understanding of Source.

As a child, often, my experiences with Spirit were dismissed as dreams, make-believe, or even ignored. This confused me, so it was easier to keep my encounters with Spirit to myself. When I was twelve, I awoke in the middle of the night to find my bedroom dark but also illuminated somehow. The radiance emanated from a being of light floating at the foot of my bed. I sat up and reached for my eyeglasses on my nightstand. Without them, I struggle to make out basic shapes. But as my hand touched my glasses, I realized I did not need them—I could see in vivid detail. I could see objects in my room (like the picture frames on my desk) more clearly than ever before.

The being glowed a bluish-white light from within. He levitated three feet from the ground, giving the illusion of height, despite being a little on the short side. He was masculine and bald, with a close-lipped smile, and his white shirt and pants seemed to flow. A sense of safety and love washed over me. I was not alarmed that an unfamiliar man was floating in my bedroom. Instead, his presence felt peaceful, natural somehow. He nodded, and without moving his mouth, he said, "Everything is going to be alright." I remember thinking, "Oh. Okay, great. Thank you." I rolled over and closed my eyes. I felt the urge to look back. I knew he was there. I could feel him.

The following day, I told my family about my transformative experience, but my parents did not take me seriously and brushed it off. My father's exact, disheartening words were: "I believe you believe that's what you saw." Although their response was not what I had hoped for or expected, I did not question the validity of my experience. Instead, I questioned my parents' wisdom—could I trust what they deemed credible or noncredible information, opinions, or teachings? Not long after the visit from the light being, my parents started the divorce process. They separated, and both of them moved away. Neither of my parents were financially stable enough to raise two children on their own, so my sister, Gwen, and I went to live with our grandparents. I was not scared because the being in my room had reassured me we would be all right.

Childhood experiences like mine occur frequently. In the West, it is common for parents to believe these experiences are an active part of their child's imagination. After a while, children keep their psychic or mystical experiences to themselves. As they age, they become increasingly unaware of their sensitivities to the unseen world around them.

It is not long before these children ignore their own intuitive experiences. As a result, they grow up dismissing their spiritual awareness because it falls outside of accepted social norms.

Connections to others, to Self, and to something greater are natural, even if we do not realize what is happening. We are never alone. I hope this book will help you understand that. We always have unseen companions around us. We are always connected to Spirit.

PART I

A-Team and Deathbed Experiences

Chapter 1

A-Team

Our world overflows with countless sounds, flavors, textures, smells, and colors. But there is more happening around us than most people are aware of—another field of information that our physical awareness does not perceive, containing thoughts, ideas, concepts, wisdom, teachings, and inspiration. It is all around us, all the time. Accessing information in this field takes practice, but we can all do it. For me, it is when I sit in solitude that I hear the Voice— my old, familiar friends in Spirit. One day, I gave my Spirit friends a collective name: *A-Team*. Months later, I informed A-Team I thought their name was lame, and I wanted to change it to something that meant "singular" or "One." I wanted it to more adequately represent a collective. "I'll look for a sign from you for an appropriate name," I said. A little later that day, I left the house to take our cat, Charlie Pancake, to the vet. Just as I arrived, a large vehicle delivered a temporary dumpster to the vet's office, blocking the parking spaces. The dumpster was olive green, and painted on the side in big, bold white letters was the word "A-Team." I laughed. I realized the letter "A" means "singular," or "one" in English, and that "A-Team" implies we are a team. I am as much a part of my collective spirit team as my spirit guides are. We need each other.

A-Team is my group of spirit guides, loved ones, inspirers, and helpers who join me in my meditative moments. It feels like their participation is both for their growth and mine, as we share a mutual gratitude. Their membership is not static—sometimes new personalities join the team. They step into my awareness with teachings relative to my life lessons and then they step back, leaving me to process the information they have shared. Sometimes I hear from them again, sometimes not. In one revealing session, it was suggested that A-Team was a group of angelic beings, ascended masters, ancestors, Arcturians, and alternate dimensional beings. I thought this was interesting since all of those word choices also started with A. There are, however, a few members of A-Team that seem ever-present. They have expressed that how they look in my mind's eye and the names I have given them are less important than their messages. But it helps me on a human level to assign these traits to them, as it seems easier to connect with them.

One of my guides is a feminine personality named Lyra who usually presents herself as a young woman with long hair. Often, she glows in a blueish light. Sometimes she shows herself as being elderly. She is calming and wise and refers to me as "Dear." Lyra is a teacher who loves learning something new, being at high-energy gatherings, and feeling excited.

Another A-Team personality is Kissinger. Almost always, he shows up in green light, revealing himself as an older gentleman with a beard. Kissinger is formal—an intellectual who values knowledge, and who appreciates structure but loves freedom. He finds it crucial to record information and presents himself toting a giant book holding documented data to assist him with his teachings. He is excellent at theorizing and encourages those he teaches to do the work and experience the "answers." He does not make learning lessons easy.

Jacob is always close by. He presents himself in a blue light, similar to Lyra's, and is middle-aged and charming. A scribe, he told me he heals hearts with words. Like Kissinger, he finds it important to record information. He is compassionate and cares for those he works with. He calls me "My dear boy," which I find odd because I am a woman, but the more I sit with Spirit, the more I realize labels are just ways of identifying packets of information so we can retain an experience and learn from it.

Timmy is yet another A-Team personality. He is a child, but wise beyond his years and filled with joy. He loves playing games and sports, swinging on swings, and making people smile. He is a little mischievous, but also generous, insightful, and inclusive. Timmy does essential work teaching gratitude and understanding.

There is a newer member of A-Team who looks alien. Her name is Wakonda. She has blue skin and big, dark eyes. While she is the average height of a human, she is not human—her head is more prominent. She has colored gems or lights on her body or dress. She said I had asked for her assistance with my verbal communication. She did not want me to focus on her appearance, but on her message.

Finally, there is Joseph. Joseph comes through in golden-white light, and often I see a circle around him. He feels angelic, exudes Love and has a different feel than the other members of A-Team. His energy feels lighter and is a little distant and more challenging to see than the rest of the team. He loves feeling others' joy and witnessing a-ha moments. He appreciates it when I acknowledge him, and has an observant, hands-off, protective energy.

When I sit in solitude, I write down the wisdom and channeled guidance from A-Team that flows through me. Often, the channeled writings are in response to personal life experiences and challenges, offering me opportunities for growth. Other times, I receive information that provides me with a greater understanding of others' circumstances. Some of the information that comes through is a commentary on universal Love and compassion. Regardless of what I experience in a channeled session with A-Team, I allow their data to shape my perspectives.

When we channel, we connect to something outside our physical focus and receive information through this connection. When I sit intending to connect to A-Team, I welcome their channeled communication by "hearing" their words in my head and "seeing" images in my mind. It feels to me like the information comes from the Universal Consciousness. Sometimes there is not a word in my vocabulary or in our limited language that suits A-Team, so they show me two or more words overlaid on top of each other, and I write them down with a simple slash separating them. They always refer to me in terms of endearment such as "Dear," "Young one," "Child," "Sweet friend," and even, "My dear boy." The wisdom they express is always beautiful, insightful, helpful, and healing.

There are also many spiritual beings ready to assist us who may not be on our team of guides. During meditative moments, I have met many wise beings, including a collective who call themselves "the Council." They offer wisdom and oversee certain aspects of our Souls' teachings. I feel as though they monitor many Souls' journeys and speak with authority (although I do not feel in any way "less than" in their presence). I get the impression there are many councils in Spirit ready to aid us when we seek their guidance.

All of us have helpers. We are never alone, and as A-Team says, "*Reach out to your team of guides. Flip that switch in your awareness or perspective.*" There are many spiritual teachers who can help those who need or want to connect to this wisdom, and many modalities, resources, and tools to assist you as you practice your channeling. Finding a way that works for you may take time, but the answers dwell within each one of us. Turning inward and reflecting on your inner truth is the key to a greater understanding.

Here is a quick exercise to help you tap into your extra-sensory awareness-or your "sixth sense."

Have a pen and paper handy. With eyes closed or open, without expectation, allow your mind to open. Often, it is easiest to do this with closed eyes to decrease distractions. Visualize that there are signals or waves carrying data flowing all around you. Set an intention to notice this field of information. Relax. Select a wave and imagine yourself merging with it. Let the wave surround you, enveloping all of you. Now, sense the information it carries within it. The information comes to you in thoughts or in sounds, or maybe you see pictures in your head. Once you have engaged with the information, take a deep breath and come back into your awareness of your physical surroundings. It is helpful to write down your experience afterward because it is easy to forget it, and looking back to see how your practice develops is beneficial.

A-Team says we create our physical lives through free will and choice and on a Higher Soul level. As creators of our experiences, it makes sense to release our need to control our environment. Instead, we can flow with it and shape it as challenges arise. This is where we learn. We are here, focused, gaining knowledge and growing on a Soul level, and we present ourselves with opportunities to do so. Challenges are difficult, of course, but somehow, we have all made it through so far. We are not unscathed, but we are still here, evolving and stepping into the truth of who we are, and exploring who we can be.

The answers lie within each of you / us based on what a particular personality or thought expression wants to experience. In those terms, there is no right or wrong answer. There is no right or wrong perspective, only varying degrees of experience, which paves the way for creating varying ideas, concepts, and thoughts, always creating and changing, but always One. Consider the game, Whack-A-Mole. Each mole pops up from its hole, each one with a unique perspective and timing. Each one is trying to avoid being whacked. We each have our own thoughts / ways. Sometimes, a player strikes us, and sometimes not. Regardless, we gain wisdom. With each of these experiences, our thoughts are molded and reinforced. Shift perspective. Who is holding the paddle?
~ A-Team

Chapter 2

But First, Compassion

Over the years, I questioned the nature of God. I asked myself, "Is there life after death? What is the meaning of life? What is our purpose? Why are religions different? In college, I absorbed as much information as possible about cultures and religions, earning a master's degree in art history and theology. *Could I find the answers to my questions in textbooks or holy books? From professors or religious leaders? Through learning about ancient art and philosophies? Through traveling?* Over years of research, I found information and ideas that resonated with me, but the answers to my questions were elusive. The more research I did, the more questions I had.

Throughout history, people have connected with Spirit. However, according to present-day conservative religiosity, for many modern religious thinkers and teachers, divine experiences are only historical phenomena, and communication with angels, spirits, and otherworldly entities ended with ancient prophets, saints, and seers. *Why*, I wondered, *is communion with Spirit not everyone's birthright?*

Our world traditions suggest there has been a rich history of Spirit communication spanning cultures and religions. For example, ancient Egyptians held spiritual ceremonies invoking the gods and sharing wisdom about life circumstances that were beyond human control. In ancient Greece, they consulted oracles to gain insight into daily concerns. Heads of state, ambassadors, and commoners alike sought the advice of the Sibyls or the Delphic Oracle. In Judaism, according to the Book of Torah, Moses channeled the Ten Commandments on top of Mount Sinai. In Christianity, Archangel Gabriel informed Mary of Nazareth that she would bear the son of God. In the seventh century, in Saudi Arabia, while meditating, Mohammad heard Archangel Gabriel instructing him on teachings from the one Creator, Allah. In twelfth-century Germany, Hildegard von Bingen, a Catholic abbess, received heavenly visions and heard music that offered her moral direction. In Tibetan Buddhism, dharma palas communicate with and influence human minds. In shamanism, which is practiced across Asia, Europe, North America, South America, and Africa, shamans commune with the living and the dead. Speaking with Spirit has been a part of our history for thousands of years. *So*, I wondered, *why is communing with Spirit frowned upon or dismissed in our Western world?* The answer is complex, and there are as many answers as there are religious beliefs. So, all we can do is trust.

All we can trust are the experiences we have had and the information that resonates within us. It is simple, but for someone striving for definitive answers, it is not enough. *If the answers are within each of us, there is no singular answer. Do we choose random ideologies, beliefs, and perspectives? How can we be sure we are deciding what is right for us?*

I worked hard to keep my spiritual search aligned with my day-to-day life and responsibilities, but when the stresses of everyday life surfaced, I found myself back in an empty bathtub, breathing and quieting my mind. This was how I developed a regular practice of bringing my focus inward, shifting my perspective, and allowing a greater understanding to unfold. Meditation was my key to immediate peace. Being in nature and painting also gave me a sense of connection and centeredness. I did not know it then, but I had begun to forge a path to greater awareness.

As I entered my mid-twenties, the distractions and responsibilities of life rose to the forefront. I worked, traveled, graduated from college, then went to graduate school. I got married, had kids, and built a home. My life centered around the everyday tasks of raising a family. I meditated sporadically, but did not prioritize connecting to Spirit. I focused on this wonderful physical life and all the extraordinary experiences it offered, both exciting and challenging. During this time, Spirit gave me space. Visits from A-Team were not regular—at least, that was my perception. I did not feel balanced, but

I was going full throttle, and appreciated the time and space to grow. After all, being focused physically is something we get to do. Taking in everything all around us is a gift.

After a while, A-Team decided it was time for us to reconnect. It was hard to ignore the constant, nagging gut feeling I had to get in touch with them. Finally, I cleaned out a tiny coat closet under my stairs and filled it with inspirational pieces just for me—a blue crystal singing bowl, comfy pillows, and my favorite candles and quotes. It became my personal meditation space. Just entering it made me feel centered and ready to tune in to Spirit.

A-Team's communications started flowing through weekly connections. During our moments of alone time, they questioned me and gave me guidance based on my life experiences. They especially encouraged me to consider new perspectives on practicing compassion for all situations and people. Compassion, they taught me, is having a sympathetic consciousness about others' distress, together with a desire to ease it. Because I was focusing on my children, Elle and Ty; my husband, Taylor; our home; and our family business, shifting perspectives was uncomfortable. It felt like everyone and everything needed my attention. However, A-Team persisted. I felt a different level of compassion unfold within me as I sat with my old Spirit friends daily.

The Buddhists have a mantra related to the Bodhisattva of compassion. In Sanskrit, it is "Om Mani Padme Hum." In English, it translates as "hail to the jewel in the lotus." *Om* stands for the ever-present, impure body and mind, the holy Spirit of the Buddha, and the sound of creation. Mani means *jewel*, symbolizing the intention to become enlightened through love, altruism, and compassion. Padme means *lotus* and is the symbol of wisdom and knowledge. *Hum* is the unity of altruism and wisdom, the intention to become enlightened, wise, and one in pure body, mind, and spirit. This mantra has many important meanings layered throughout its six syllables: om ma ni pad me hum. It states that we are all connected, and that there is wisdom, compassion, and understanding in each of us, hidden like the lotus under layers of mud. Compassion is a foundation for forming connections in our human experience. We are all lotus flowers with compassionate inner wisdom tucked away under life's challenges.

Compassion, as a cornerstone of our human condition, weaves together individual interactions between people. It softens our judgments of others and leaves room for understanding and new ways of seeing familiar situations. Allowing ourselves to be compassionate not only broadens our own concepts and points of view but it creates a bridge of connection to others and helps them realize they are cared for, validated, and worthy. When a person feels valued, they open themselves up to hope and new possibilities. Being compassionate is vital if we are to be inclusive, accepting, and understanding.

Compassion, my friend, is an act from the heart. It is free of preconceptions, the should and should not, and presents as a gentle nudge of support. Compassion is free of hierarchy, seeing each Soul as equal and deserving. It is an approach to better understanding others and ourselves, reminding us of our inner connection and vulnerabilities. Compassion can ease judgments, aggressions, guilt, and blame, as it is a spotlight of truth, shedding light on the reality of the present moment—the now.

~ A-Team

Chapter 3

Dean

The death of my father, Dean, affected me profoundly. In fact, I credit his death as jumpstarting me to serve the dying community. Dad enjoyed watching sports, relaxing in his recliner, and drinking rum and Coke. Over the years, his drinking habits increased, leading to cirrhosis of the liver, but he was a private man and kept his failing health to himself. He lived alone in a mobile home on a ranch, receiving few visitors. In rare moments of vulnerability, he expressed his fear of dying on the property and not being found for days.

One fall, Dad came to visit me and my family. We were happy to see him, but found his presence challenging. As the day arrived for him to go home, he announced he would stay with us longer. He refused to admit it, but I knew it was because he had been drinking all morning, hiding his alcohol in a Styrofoam coffee cup, and did not want to get behind the wheel of his truck. This happened again the following morning. His inability to stay sober long enough to drive home concerned me and Taylor. Dad sat on the couch watching the news at top volume all day. He had brought his dog (which was inconvenient because we had cats) and he littered our yard with cigarette butts. He did not take suggestions well, and because we had not established firm boundaries of behavior or expectations, I became irritated. I did not want to make him feel unwelcome. So, I escaped to my coat closet under the stairs. I attempted to clear my thoughts and said a prayer for Dad. As I did, I had a vision—a subtle but powerful, transformative experience. I saw the colors red and black, heard the word "decay," and saw my father dying in a hospital bed. The number 5 was flashing above his head. The room was bright, with bluish aqua walls. I sensed others in the room behind me as I stood next to him, and my daughter, Elle, held my hand, observing.

When I snapped back to physical reality, I felt a sense of dread and discomfort. But I also had a knowing that it made sense and was as it should be. I journaled my vision and told Taylor and a neighbor about my impressions. When someone receives such a vision, it can be confusing. *Is it a premonition? My imagination? A possibility or a probability? Can I change the outcome, or is it predetermined?* Dad left that week, and while I was ready for him to go, looking back, I am grateful for the time with him.

In the coming months, I focused on the kids' school year, extracurricular activities, and the upcoming holidays. When we gathered for Christmas in what would be the last months of Dad's life, his physical appearance had changed drastically—it was clear he was sick. After a small intervention, he agreed to enter a month-long rehabilitation program. Our family met with a therapist who specializes in rehabilitation and substance abuse. He warned us that some patients do not make it out of rehab even after detox. Their health is too compromised. Those words foreshadowed the following events.

On weekends, the center opened for family visits. On one visit, Dad hugged me and said, "Thank you, honey. Thank you for doing this." It was heartwarming to know that he felt good about himself and was stronger for being sober for two weeks. He had always been a loner, but he made friends in rehab and the camaraderie eased his loneliness.

On another visit to see Dad with my grandmother, Sylvia (whom we called "Grandmom"), and my sister, Gwen, Dad was not as pleasant. He was being obstinate, and Grandmom was being firm with him. Suddenly, his deceased father, Bob (whom we called "Grandbob"), appeared behind him. Grandbob looked amazing. He was a younger, healthier version of himself. His hands were resting on Dad's shoulders. He laughed and commented on our conversations. At one point, I heard him say, "Drop the hammer (and an inaudible word)," to Grandmom. I blurted out, "Grandbob's here." My family stared at me, said nothing, and continued their conversation. Grandbob brought with him pure joy, love, and excitement, and he stayed until our visit ended. After we left, Grandmom asked me about seeing Grandbob. She surmised that the "inaudible word" Grandbob had said was "Kid," his nickname for her. "Drop the hammer" was Grandbob's way of saying "You tell him, Kid." It was also significant because my grandparents collected antique hammers and tools. I felt relieved that she believed me. Grandmom's open-minded attitude made me question why I had not confided my experiences with Spirit with her sooner.

A week and a half later, we received a call around 10:00 p.m. The healthcare providers in the facility had found my dad in his room, confused, with a fever. They sent him to their local hospital, where the staff kept Grandmom and my aunt and uncle apprised of his condition by phone, and they made decisions to help him survive. Gwen and I drove two hours to the hospital. Grandmom, my aunt and uncle, and my sister, Victoria, came from further south; they had a six-hour trip.

The drive to be at a dying loved one's side can feel slow. As I focused on the road ahead, Dad appeared in the car to my left and said, "This is my choice." At that moment, I felt transported to another space or awareness, and I understood he was dying. I knew it was all in divine order. I was not sad; it simply was. I was driving my car, but simultaneously I was in this other space, connecting with Dad somewhere only a few feet higher than where I sat. It was a place of peace. His words rang true, and I respected his choice. It was as if all was perfect and as it should be. I told him I loved him. As he faded from my perception, I noticed my surroundings inside my car. My human side stepped back in, wanting to shout, "No. Wait, you can't go… not yet!" Another part of me wondered, *Was I really just in two places at once?* Minutes later, we received the phone call: Dad had passed away. My sister, Victoria, said she thought Dad had just hugged her. I told her he had been with me and Gwen, too. I shared my experience of Dad showing up in the car with us moments earlier.

Loved ones who have transitioned can allow those of us still in physical form to feel their presence. These experiences can come in as a knowing, a scent, a feeling of being touched, or you can even hear words or phrases spoken in the same cadence as the dearly departed. These moments may only last a few seconds but can feel longer, leaving the bereaved feeling loved and a little lighter.

At the hospital, they took me to see Dad. I sat down to meditate. "Are you still here, Dad?" I asked. I heard him say, "I'm here, honey,"… plain as day. Tears of pain and joy streamed down my face. When the rest of my family arrived, we did all the logistical paperwork the hospital needed. Then, in disbelief, we started our return trip home. As we drove, my neighbor called to express her condolences and reminded me that I had told her about my vision months before.

My father passed away 5 months after that vision, on February 5th, 2015, at 57… all those fives. That was why the "5" had flashed above Dad's head. He died from complications of liver cirrhosis: *decay*. The hospital walls were a blueish-aqua color. Since it was only five months after the premonition, Elle still looked the same age as she had been in my vision. This prophetic perception increased my trust in Spirit and myself. I started paying closer attention. *Are the visions meant to be informative? Are they given to us so we can change circumstances?* I started focusing my awareness on free choice, destiny, and preordained paths.

Dad, not an excellent communicator in life, proved to be a phenomenal one in death. He came through loud and clear in my meditations. When Gwen was due for a second brain surgery after Dad's passing, he reassured me he would be there. He had been an integral part of her first surgery, advocating for her when she struggled to do so for herself. "Not even death can keep me from being there," he said. I relayed his message to Gwen. Knowing he would be there gave her a little peace.

On the day of Gwen's surgery, I went into my meditation closet and updated Dad on Gwen. I told him we needed a sign to help bring peace and hope that he was still there for Gwen. I heard him say, "I'm here." I dismissed his words. "No, Dad, I need more than that." I felt him hug me. I loved that hug. It was almost as if he was there in the closet with me. I was grateful, but wanted a bigger sign, something that would help me know I was not making it all up. "Do better, Dad," I said.

Taylor needed help in the office. I walked down the hall and, as I approached my desk, a picture of Dad fell off the shelf and landed on my keyboard. That had never happened before, (and it never happened again). I cried and said, "Okay, Dad, I know you're here. Be with Gwen. She needs you. You'll love being in the surgery room this time."

During Gwen's recovery, she and Mom stayed with me. We were playing board games and laughing when an old mantle-sized grandfather clock (the kind you have to wind) started chiming. In fifteen years, that was the only time that clock ever chimed. We all looked at each other. We knew it was Dad.

This experience taught me that our loved ones want to let us know they are near just as much as we want to know they are still here. It also taught me we all have options in our physical life and, many times, in the timing of our physical death. When Dad told me, "It's my choice," his words shifted my perspectives on death. I know Dad, as a personality, would not have chosen to die in his earthly life, but his Soul chose to die. This has helped me grasp the concept and accept the mystery of why some people die when they do.

Spirit says life is eternal. So there is no actual death. The physical body changes form, but there is no death of who we are. We are a Soul, a multi-faceted Being choosing many experiences for the sake of learning and growing... perhaps even just for the joy of it! Our experiences, while we have free will, are orchestrated for the greatest good for ourselves and the Whole. No One dies.

Referring to one's ability to choose outcomes around their bodily death, there are many scenarios to consider. Some cooperate on a Soul level as part of what they deem necessary as retribution or as an act of fairness or balance. Others choose it to express or bring awareness to a compassionate opportunity. Some are aware it is their time and want to leave in a blaze of glory, and others have different reasons. Regardless, every Soul takes part in their death. Of course, there is no real death.

~ A-Team

Chapter 4

Death Doula Work Is Social Awareness

Through the gentle nudges of Spirit, I have been exploring perspectives on compassion by volunteering in my community. Working alongside young and old people, able-bodied and disabled people, as well as the disadvantaged and the sick, I have gained a greater understanding of life as others view it. Serving others starts with empathy. Often, people ask themselves, "What would I do in someone else's shoes?" or "How can I become more empathetic?" Spirit clarifies that rather than asking what we should do differently, we should try to *feel* what others are experiencing. Our empathy will bring us a greater understanding of their situation. Empathy is the foundation for all compassionate connections—and everyone needs connection.

In our human condition, we yearn to feel we are a part of a greater whole, a part of something bigger than ourselves. We want to belong to a family, a club, a neighborhood, a community, or a country. We adapt our behavior, make choices to please others, and set our needs aside, hoping others will like and accept us. When we are children, this behavior is essential for survival. We observe our environment and adapt to established family norms. Often, we sacrifice our authenticity to keep the peace and to feel appreciation, love, and inclusion. Having learned how to fit in, as we grow up, we take on roles that identify us as what we do and how we contribute rather than who we are at our core.

When we alter our behavior for a group, we determine what we think the group's needs are. We judge others' choices and compare them to our own decisions. Our actions stem from a place of fear that others will not accept us, instead of from the heart-centered knowledge that we already belong. What if we could set our preconceived, competitive notions aside and honor our authentic selves through compassion, empathy, and understanding? How beautifully interesting and diverse we could all be without shame or fear!

To teach empathy and compassion on a broad scale requires social transformation. Social justice movements throughout history have called attention to the inequality between different social classes in our communities. Social class, gender, age, sexual orientation, and race are all embedded in our societies. The suffrage movement, child labor laws, the Civil Rights Act, the agricultural worker's movement, the fight for transgender and gay rights, and the Black Lives Matter movement, to name a few, each call for empathy. To help the broader community recognize social injustice, these movements encourage others to shift their perspectives and see other members of society through a lens of equality. We are all experiencing life from individual vantage points. How can we grow without challenges and without learning new ideas? When we understand the experiences of others are just as important as our own, our eyes open to the beautifully diverse world we live in together.

Being brave enough to imagine ourselves in someone else's shoes exposes us to different perspectives and helps us relate to others. The more views we can imagine and adopt, the more we will cease to judge, and the more our understanding will increase. We will treat others equitably.

Another less radical way to increase social awareness is to work with an organization that helps people, witnessing first-hand the difference they make in the lives they serve. It is joyous to watch someone light up when they speak about a passion, a life's dream, or a reality they have manifested with the help of a charity or non-profit. Taking part in the experiences offered by these organizations sparks gratitude and is humbling. While I find it fulfilling to help people and groups who are creating a better quality of life, I also feel compelled to understand how people can create a better-quality death.

Standing beside someone who is experiencing a devastating, life-altering situation can be heart-wrenching. Fear and hopelessness are all-encompassing, and one cannot help but want to ease those feelings. I wanted to bring peace to others—to help ease their fears and offer a sense of hope to those in desperate situations. So given my ability to connect with the Spirit world, I focused on aiding those who are afraid of dying and death. I found myself called to sit with patients close to death because I wanted them to know there is nothing to fear. To help them find peace, I became certified as a Death Doula.

Also called an End-of-Life Doula, Death Doulas help those at the end of their life transition. Besides working with private clients, I volunteer at local hospices and with a group called NODA. NODA is an acronym for a hospital-based program called "No One Dies Alone." NODA volunteers sit with patients who do not have family and would otherwise be alone in their last days.

While I hoped my work with hospices and NODA would connect me with patients in a way they might find comforting, these experiences brought me comfort, too. Patients see loved ones surrounding them, they see angels, and often they show themselves stepping out of their bodies and interacting in such a way that I feel an overwhelming sense of Love, freedom, and expansiveness. While our human mind may perceive suffering in the dying process, the Soul is joyous. I am so grateful for these experiences. I know we are never alone, and that truly, life is eternal.

Unfortunately, death is a taboo subject and rarely do we discuss it without it having a sad or unlucky connotation. Western culture finds death uncomfortable, scary, and tragic. Often, people seem to believe we have more time than we do, and to many people, death comes as a surprise. Death is unavoidable. It comes for the sick, the healthy, the elderly, and the young. It can strike without warning or be a welcome end to long-term pain and suffering. Because we give little thought to our deaths, we are not prepared when our time comes. We spend our lives knowing we have our whole lives ahead of us and, year after year, we believe there is another year left.

Because we live as if we will never die, we put off doing things we hope to do. As death approaches, we find ways to "fight" death through modern medicine and technology, and sometimes, we buy a bit more time. But often, people spend their extra time dying more instead of living more. Rarely do we live out the rest of our days doing things we always wanted to do. Instead, we die slowly and fight harder, hoping for more time to die.

We could treat our unavoidable death as an expected transition, a passing of consciousness from the physical realm to a nonphysical one. The day of our death is a day family and friends can surround, support, and revere us, just like they did on the day we were born. Grief is natural. We will miss our loved ones; we will long for their hugs, kisses, touch, laughter, and support. But there is solace in offering and honoring our loved ones with a good death.

As my involvement with dying clients increased, so did my interactions with their families and friends. Initially, I helped them develop coping skills and provided a sympathetic ear to support them in processing their immediate grief. However, my role gradually evolved into guiding the bereaved to find a greater purpose and gain fresh perspectives on the rest of their lives. Frequently, I sit with A-Team and jot down the wisdom they share with clients seeking honest, centered guidance. This experience provides comfort and helps them set their expectations for their own eventual death. It also helps their families gain peace for the future.

Serving the dying community and those in need of a little guidance has been more rewarding than I could have imagined. The service and its reward are two sides of the same coin. Both the dying and their loved ones need understanding—non-judgmental, compassionate connections—and hope. These heart-centered interactions transpire best when I simply listen. When I give people the opportunity to express themselves, their inner wisdom heals their hearts. Everyone knows on a Soul level what they need most. Listening allows them to figure it out on their own. These a-ha moments change people from the inside out.

When I started this work, I believed I was providing a service for my clients, but as I said, I benefit from these experiences as well.

I learn about life from the perspective of someone on their deathbed. People share their hopes and dreams with me as they prepare to cope with grief and loss. When a loved one passes, the bereaved must come to terms with what has occurred, as often, what they imagined would happen in their future is no longer their reality. The awareness of a loved one's impending death can shift our perspective on time and make us feel rushed, as the grief of unfulfilled goals and regrets surfaces. I listen to shifts in thoughts as patients and their loved one's process and accept their fast-approaching fate.

Working at the bedsides of those who are dying allows me to witness and share the spiritual experiences my clients and their families have. I have them, too. These ever-evolving experiences shape my convictions and faith. Everyone has a perspective and a belief system based on their personal experience. Even a belief in nothing is a belief in something, and that belief shapes our decisions and points of view.

In this book, I share some of my clients' stories. I hope that reading them will broaden your perspective about death, and help you gain a better understanding of what you want and do not want for yourself when death approaches.

> *Death itself is inevitable. She is the great equalizer/balancer. She is a humbling friend who forces one to explore the deepest crevices, perceptions, dreams, and desires of one's Soul. She is merciful but appears merciless under limiting views/eyes. Her breath of death gives life. Life takes on a new form, a new understanding. She waits patiently, watching. She has no regrets; she knows she is the usher of new life and change. She loves her work, for she is a great healer, a great transformer. Give thanks to her, for where would we be without her?*
> *~ A-Team*

Chapter 5

Mrs. Julie

One spring morning, A-Team shared some news. I was to meet a new client soon, a woman with cancer, who was to be admitted to a nearby nursing home. They said I would benefit from our time together. I waited for the call that would place me in the path of someone who turned out to be one of my favorite clients. I will call her Mrs. Julie.

Doctors diagnosed Mrs. Julie with terminal brain cancer. Because Gwen has had brain cancer, this hit home: I know the physical, emotional, and spiritual toll this disease can take. Mrs. Julie's wife requested caregivers not tell her of her impending death because the news would be too devastating. As an End-of-Life-Doula, this was challenging. How could I bring Mrs. Julie peace, awareness, and acceptance if I could not tell her she was dying?

As I arrived at the nursing home, eager to meet my new client, I noticed the heaviness in the facility. The energy was thick, slow, and dense. As I strolled through the hall, looking for Mrs. Julie's room number, I felt the stares of the many sick patients as I passed by. I flashed a brief, sympathetic smile to them, wondering, *What are they thinking?* I was aware of my swift stride and effortless movements, while in their frail bodies, they struggled to stand up or sit down.

I found Mrs. Julie's room. I took a deep breath and entered. "Hi. You must be Mrs. Julie," I said.

"Yeah," she responded.

"I'm Gretchen. If it's okay with you, I'd love to visit you a few times a week."

"Okay. That would be fine," she replied.

I pulled up a chair. We stared at each other. She had thin, dark hair growing back from chemo treatments and wore a pair of small, wire-framed glasses. I asked, "How do you feel in your new space?"

"I'm only here until my back heals," she said. "I fell, but I don't remember how."

From what I knew from Gwen's experiences with brain cancer, I thought a seizure must have caused her fall. I glanced around the bare clinical room. Compared to the other rooms in the facility (brimming with pictures, cozy bedding, cards, and mementos), her room was stark. Mrs. Julie was a little uncomfortable, but she was also curious and welcomed a visitor. We engaged in small talk, but there were many moments of silence between us. I left our initial meeting feeling like Mrs. Julie might be a challenge.

Knowing I could not discuss her terminal condition with her, in the following week I made her space a bit more comforting. I brought fabric to hang on the walls, a clock, a blanket, and a speaker so I could play music from my cell phone playlists. Mrs. Julie's wife had delivered a flat-screen TV.

As I walked into her room, Mrs. Julie sat up and smoothed her hair. She asked me to open up the top drawer of her nightstand. Inside, I found a blonde costume wig and handed it to her. She put it on and smiled. "Do I look nice?" she asked.

"Yes," I said, and smiled. I took her picture with my phone and showed it to her.

"Oh yeah. I look good," she said.

During this second visit, Mrs. Julie opened up to me. She loved the Avengers, coloring books, game shows, Reese's peanut butter cups, Jesus, and country music. She complained she was losing her ability to see clearly. I cleaned her glasses, which cured her fuzzy vision. I made a point of cleaning her glasses every time I visited, and being able to see gave her an instant mood boost. She was starting to like me.

On subsequent visits, I brought Mrs. Julie Reese's peanut butter cups, an Avengers coloring book, and a battery-operated, fake-flame Jesus candle. Mrs. Julie loved the Jesus candle. I turned it on and set it on her bed tray. To her, the flickering flame was mesmerizing, magical.

It brought her joy and inspired her to lead us in prayer. She stared at Jesus's face on the candle, and it was as if she were speaking to Him directly. Her prayers were always heartfelt, thoughtful, and loving. We both looked forward to her prayers and her words of appreciation for those she loved.

Mrs. Julie enjoyed coloring. She did not have a favorite color, so at each visit, she chose one marker and colored the entire page that color. I hung her art on the wall, and that delighted her. She loved watching all her favorite shows on television. She warmed up to our visits, and we called each other friends. "I don't have any other friends," she told me. "My partner is my only family."

After about six weeks, I noticed a decline in Mrs. Julie's vocabulary and her ability to recall events. She could no longer hold a marker and her fine motor skills were deteriorating, so she lost interest in coloring. One of the few routine activities she still found peace in was the prayer she led at the start of our visits admiring the magical flame of the Jesus candle. Even with her frail movements and increasing lethargy, she still found strength to praise Jesus for what she had.

Frequently, Mrs. Julie stared off into space—a sign she was having a minor seizure. One afternoon, we were watching *The Price Is Right*, and she had one of these seizures. "Do you think my tumor has returned?" she asked. "It has. I just know it."

Her question surprised me. "Maybe, because your seizure activity has increased. What do you think that means?" I asked.

"I don't know," she mumbled.

We continued watching *The Price Is Right* in silence. After a while, Mrs. Julie looked at me and said, "I'm going to be taking a train ride soon."

Such moments are examples of a phenomenon called "nearing-death awareness." Nearing-death awareness occurs in some patients when they know death is near, but they cannot explain what they know or how they know it. Sometimes they make travel references, such as saying they are taking a trip, waiting for a bus or a plane, or (as in Mrs. Julie's case) going on a train ride. Sometimes families brush off these statements as confusion, and sometimes medical staff administer medication to treat end-of-life delirium. Family members may try to convince their loved ones they are not going on a trip and attempt to bring them back to reality. But recognizing the signs of nearing-death awareness can be an amazing opportunity to prepare the patient (and ourselves) for a peaceful, aware death.

"Where are you going?" I asked. "How long will you be gone and when are you leaving?"

"I don't know, but I know it's soon," she responded.

"Have you ever been on a train?"

"No."

I pressed her about her faith. "What do you think happens after death?"

"I believe in a heaven where I will see my parents and my pets. I'll see Jesus and I'll live forever in the sky filled with love."

In an attempt to gauge her awareness of her impending death, I continued our conversation without revealing her terminal prognosis directly by stating that, "Nobody knows when they will die. It could be today, tomorrow, or even a year from now."

She agreed. We talked about how knowing when you will die is not as important as knowing that when you do, it is okay. This was one way I could speak of death as natural and help her accept it, without revealing to her she had a terminal illness.

As Mrs. Julie declined, she slipped into younger, child-like behaviors. She found joy in her daily activities and simple pleasures. By this time, we had an established routine for our visits. I came in, said hello, and turned on the Jesus candle. She'd look at the magic flame excitedly and lead us in a thoughtful, heart-felt prayer. Then I would offer her a Reese's peanut butter cup. She would take a bite, then another and another. "Oh, yeah, that's good," she would say with every single bite. Listening to her eat her Reese's peanut butter cups always made me laugh. Finally, we would talk or watch TV together.

Often, Mrs. Julie mentioned her wife did not visit her as often or for as long as she'd like. She felt lonely. This is a recurring comment my clients make. As their physical death draws near, time spent with family never seems like enough. They feel the need to have family and friends close, and they miss them the moment they leave.

One afternoon, the facility called to tell me that Mrs. Julie had suffered a grand mal seizure and was unresponsive. I rushed to see her. They had moved her to an empty clinical room. She lay there, all alone, motionless. I talked to her, but she did not reply. A nurse came in and told me that Mrs. Julie had not come around and not to be disappointed if she did not respond to my words. I appreciated her attempts to manage my expectations. I prayed for Mrs. Julie's smooth transition and set intentions that she be guided through her process peacefully. I laid my hands on her while I said a prayer to comfort her. She groaned, her eyelids fluttered, and she opened her eyes. Astonished, I centered myself in front of her so she could see me clearly. She stared through me, past me.

"It's okay to go," I told her. I brought out the Jesus candle and turned it on. I held it in her line of sight, and to my amazement, her eyes locked on it. "Would you like to say a prayer?" I asked.

She nodded.

"Would you like me to lead us?" I asked. She never had wanted me to lead our prayer before.

She shook her head. She shifted her gaze toward me—but all she could say was "Da."

After what felt like a full minute of her repeating, "Da," I interrupted. "Even if you feel frustrated about not getting your words out, Jesus knows what you are saying in your heart."

She nodded and continued her single-sound prayer for a few more minutes. Finally, she ended her prayer, "Da-da," (A-men). She closed her eyes. She was unresponsive.

I left her side, knowing it would be the last time I would see her.

Later, while I was out running errands, Mrs. Julie appeared in the passenger seat of my car. I felt her gratitude and appreciation. Then she was gone. The experience lasted only seconds, but it overwhelmed me with a deep, loving, heart-felt connection. To this day, I am so grateful for that moment. Although I already knew, I called the care home to check in on her and got the news that Mrs. Julie had passed away.

I learned from Mrs. Julie, just as A-Team said I would. I learned that even in debilitating moments, such as when a person is bedridden, in pain, and has no control over their day, seeing the positive in the little things can keep them upbeat. Mrs. Julie found joy in rooting for game show contestants to win big and she relished every bite of those Reese's peanut butter cups. Mrs. Julie relinquished control easily, letting go of expectations and time frames for her healing which many people struggle to do. In doing so, she found peace and acceptance in her new routine, all the while hoping she could go home.

Mrs. Julie made me realize that so often, while the rest of the world is going about their day, dying patients are stuck, unable to reach out and visit their loved ones. They miss their friends and family. The time a family member schedules to stop by is cherished beyond words and is never enough for the patient. To those who are dying, time is the most valuable thing, and the quality of time they spend with loved ones cannot be topped.

Even though Mrs. Julie never said she was dying, I learned that a person's heart, on a Soul level, knows when death is near. They feel it, and in Mrs. Julie's case, she talked about it in a roundabout way by sharing that she would be taking a train ride. This helped her to prepare and accept what is inevitable for all of us. I loved Mrs. Julie for the beautiful innocence she lived by and for the confidence she had within herself, despite her health.

Open your eyes and see beyond what is before you to reveal the flame of truth, illuminating a perspective that shines from within.
~ A-Team

Chapter 6

Shared Death Experiences

It has been my great joy to witness spiritual events at the bedside of dying clients. These encounters have affected me profoundly and leave me with a strong sense of knowing all is as it should be, that everything is okay, and that there is so much more to life than our physical existence. These experiences are available to everyone. The key to being a part of such events is being open to them, setting an intention, quieting your mind, and being mindful of your dying loved one.

These shared-death spiritual events do not have to take place at the bedside of the person you love. You can be in another room, another city, even across the world. Time and space do not matter. The beauty, acceptance, and connection that flow through these incredible moments are gifts for and from the Soul. We never forget them. They affect us on a core level.

Shared death experiences are important because they help us understand death and dying and assist us in realizing our Souls are eternal. They help us release anxiety, calm our fear of the unknown, and ease our discomfort about the process of dying. They bring us peace and help us know that, even in death, we are not alone. We will see our loved ones again, just as our dying loved one sees those who transitioned before them welcoming them back to the Spirit world.

Death is not the last goodbye, and shared death experiences help us embrace this truth as we make the journey from grief to healing. Knowing there is eternal life brings hope for continued relationships and soothes our desperate feelings of loss.

Sometimes bedside spiritual experiences happen spontaneously, but it helps to believe that such events are possible. Otherwise, the brain can filter out non-physical phenomena. Otherworldly encounters happen around us all the time but comprehending them takes practice. Learning to meditate and turn inward is a great start.

This exercise assists you in understanding what it feels like to shift, connect beyond the physical world, and become aware of the Spirit world and other dimensions? Here is an exercise that will help you tap into the Spirit world an experience the shift for yourself:

This is an exercise in being in two worlds at once. Take a moment and close your eyes. Imagine yourself at a familiar location. Focus on the details of that place. For example, imagine standing at the beach. Listen to the rush of the waves crashing onto the shore. Hear the cry of a seagull. Notice the gritty sand beneath your feet. Feel the salty sea breeze blowing through your hair.

Now, notice the physical space you are in right now. Feel the seat in which you are sitting. Hear the sounds around you. During this practice, you are mindful of two separate places at once. You are aware of the space that surrounds you and you are aware of another space too, one that is slightly distant from your physical self: the beach. You can hear the waves, feel the sand, and feel your seat. You are experiencing two worlds at once.

Becoming aware of the Spirit world and your physical world simultaneously can feel imagined at first, but practice strengthens discernment and you will become more confident about otherworldly awareness.

Often, we dismiss an experience with Spirit because the impression is so subtle. It can feel like a thought or even a voice in your head that sounds just like you. It can feel fleeting, like a word on the tip of your tongue or a whisper you cannot interpret. Spirit is always there, ready for you to tune in to it. After all, as A-Team explains, we are all right *here*. There is no *there*. Focused in physical form or not, we are all right *here*. Wherever we choose to focus, that is where we are.

A friend explained to me once that interpreting Spirit is like running information through a radio antenna. We receive information from this other dimension, but we can also send information out to Spirit, asking for help, guidance, or even a sign. As the receiver, we are fine-tuning our frequency to get a better signal and a stronger connection. Just because we cannot see radio waves or ultraviolet light does not mean they are not there. It is the same with Spirit.

Spirit tried once to help me understand the empty space we see between people or objects is not empty at all. Our perception is that there is only air, but really, layers of information we cannot perceive fill the space. Spirit told me to imagine light refractions and reflections in and on water when we are swimming. They do not obstruct our movement. We can move right through them. Still, they are there, interacting with our reality, two separate worlds in the same space. These worlds collide yet continue on their respective journeys unaffected.

Because the Spirit world *is* our world, and because we *are* Spirit, connecting with another Soul or Spirit from another plane of existence is natural. Shared death experiences offer loved ones a fleeting glimpse of seeing beyond our physical world and into the next. Such experiences are beautiful and offer a sense of eternal connection. They include (but are not limited to) seeing your loved one outside their physical body; seeing angels, bright lights, or beings of light; feeling as though you are being transported to another space; or having a sudden knowing or awareness that a loved one has transitioned to spirit. While these are just a few examples, every experience brings a level of peace, awareness, and understanding, often leaving the loved one affected feeling grateful for the gift of the shared death experience.

What if you strive to have a shared death experience and do not have one? It can be discouraging to discover that someone else hardly tried and experienced a shared death phenomenon at a loved one's bedside. It is unclear why certain people have them and others do not. So, if you hold vigil at a dying person's bedside and do not have a shared death experience, this does not mean you cannot have one. It simply means you did not have one during this person's death. Some researchers believe that the person who needs healing and personal growth the most will have a shared death experience. Others suggest that to have a shared death experience, you must possess a certain level of spiritual open-mindedness. Whatever the reality, it is important to remember that death is a part of life, and when we die, we move our focus from this dense physical reality to another, lighter reality.

It is beautiful to be a part of a loved one's departure. It would be an amazing gift if everyone who desired it could experience a shared death experience and a heartfelt goodbye. Life on Earth could hold even more wonder.

When you ask to blend with a personality, you are asking to become aware of the experiences held dear and learned from. You are becoming aware of the information web all around you, thoughts included.
~ A-Team

Chapter 7

John

My Grandpa John was a handy, creative, loyal person. He could fix or build almost anything, from chicken coops to tables. He loved painting landscapes and when he could not afford canvases, he painted smooth rocks he collected on his walks. His loyalty to family and country was admirable. One of his most important jobs was taking part in raising his grandkids. He cared for stray animals and feeding the birds in his yard was a priority. Frequently, he sang and whistled, and on rare occasions, played his harmonica. He loved to dress up and took pride in his appearance. His life was busy, something was always going on, and the house was always full.

As Grandpa got older, his patience with life's challenges decreased. He was tired, and he did not have the energy to fix others' problems anymore. After a series of health issues, he deteriorated, and soon kidney failure was his top concern. He relied on help from my grandmother and Gwen to move around and tend to his needs. He received regular dialysis for his kidneys, hoping to regain his health. He loathed the treatments.

Then we discovered Grandpa had liver cancer, and it had spread. The news was heartbreaking, but not unexpected. My family encouraged him to continue with dialysis, hoping to prolong his life, but Grandpa asked his doctor, if dialysis will help with his prognosis, the answer was "No." Grandpa decided not to receive treatment that day. He went home, accepted hospice care, and made the choice to die. Upon hearing the news, many family members arrived to be by his side. I was in Texas, and Grandpa was in Arizona. I arranged childcare and booked a flight leaving two days later. But I did not use the ticket—Grandpa John died the following day.

Time and space do not interfere with connections during a death. When I realized Grandpa had entered the phase of actively dying and it was likely I would not be by his side, I set up a vigil for him in my home in Texas. I went into a quiet room where I could relax away from distractions. I dimmed the lights, got comfortable, and started with prayer. I prayed for peace, awareness, and a fearless, pain-free bodily death for Grandpa. I prayed he would transition in a manner that aligned with his highest, greatest good. I knew my intention had power and sent him compassionate, loving, peaceful thoughts. It was not long before I became aware of Grandpa's energy, and I connected to him easily. I sensed his readiness and impatience. I sat quietly, feeling and observing in a positive, grateful way.

Grandpa's deceased father, Pa John, showed up in Spirit in front of me. I had never met Pa John in my earthly life but had met him many times in Spirit, so I recognized him right away. He presented himself with two other Spirits, one flanking each side of him. I knew one of the Spirits with him was my Great Uncle Percy, but could not tell who the other one was. They gave me the impression of great excitement and urgency at the same time. Pa John positioned himself with his back to me. Turning toward me, he said, "We're with Grandpa, and we have to go now." This helped me understand that Grandpa's transition was imminent, and that Pa John, Great Uncle Percy, and the other Spirit person were his welcoming committee.

I called my family out west and reported my experience. Not long after that, Grandpa slipped into a state I call "aware but unconscious." This happens often when people notice their impending transition and shift their mental focus from this material world to the Spirit world. They are aware they are in more than one reality at once, and their personality prepares for the transition. It is helpful when those at the bedside understand the dying person is not hallucinating or confused at this stage—they are experiencing another distinct reality. Some people, unaware of this shift, try to interpret the experience in a logical-earthly sense instead of letting things flow. And sometimes, as noted earlier, caregivers medicate the dying person. If you are with someone when this phase of dying occurs, consider it an opportunity to walk your loved one through one of the most critical, valuable, uplifting, and empowering times in life.

Mom told me later that Grandpa appeared to be talking to others in the room whom my family could not see. He was saying, "Help me." This was distressing to everyone because they assumed he was begging for help to ease his pain and suffering. They felt a compassionate need to help but felt helpless. Then Mom realized he was not in agony—he was asking Spirit to assist him in leaving his body. He was ready to go. Mom sensed a deep knowing of this truth—and it relieved the family's stress.

Still in an aware but unconscious state, Grandpa declared, "Yes, Sir!" in a stand-at-attention, military style. Mom knew he was speaking to Pa John. Both were military men.

When Grandpa transitioned, it was a sad moment for us, but his loved ones in spirit greeted him and welcomed him back. In my vision, he grabbed Pa John's hand, and they merged in a celebratory hug. Grandpa's relief, lightness, and the joy he and Pa John shared were palpable. He had left his dense physical body behind and I was grateful that Grandpa and Spirit allowed me to share in his departure. I felt his love, and I knew he could feel my love, too. The experience felt right, in flow with life, and I knew everything was okay.

That is a gift of a shared death experience. Although I was over two thousand miles away, I could still assist in Grandpa's transition. I prayed, set my intention, and "tuned in" to him, which meant focusing my love and thoughts on him and on something greater than myself. Whether you call it the Spirit World, Heaven, the Other Side, or Across the Veil, all these terms suggest the same place. But remember, that place is here, right here where you are now. When we leave our physical bodies, we are still here, seeing a reality no longer limited by the rods and cones of our eyes. We experience our lives differently than in a human body, but it is still life, ongoing in a distinct vibration.

We are all connected through Love; all of us. We are all one and made of Love, so that is the frequency to which we all relate at a core level. You are always connected. Focus your attention, and you will feel this deep link.

~ A-Team

Chapter 8

Support of Our Dying

In my years of serving the dying community, I have found it best to release expectations around how we want death to unfold for our dying family members. It is helpful to know what our family member wants and to remain open to inspiration and resources throughout the process. Often, expected deaths occur in unexpected or inconvenient moments. It can be difficult, for example, when a caregiver learns their loved one has transitioned at the moment they stepped out of the room, even though they sat bedside for days. Weather or traffic-related incidents can keep loved ones from delivering the bedside care they had hoped to give, and death can occur just as a person holding vigil nods off to sleep. In such circumstances, watchful loved ones can feel guilty for not being present for the dying person's last breath.

People who are dying have some control over when they transition. Some people will hold out as long as possible for a loved one to arrive at their bedside. Others prefer to pass when no one is watching to spare their loved ones the anguish of witnessing a last breath. There is no need to emphasize the body's last exhale. The journey up to that point is just as important, as is the journey after it. The last breath is just the final moment before the body lets go—a person's Soul is likely already separating from their body and observing the process. The body is like a vehicle. We hop in it for a little while. Some of us take it fast, others slow. Some run it into the ground, and others take it in for regular maintenance. But regardless of the way we choose to live, eventually our bodies will die, and when that happens, we hop out. We do not have to stay in it until it putters out. We can watch from outside the vehicle as it coasts to a stop.

The last breath is not the defining moment of a good death. The days, weeks, months, and even years leading up to death are important, too. We can be helpful to our dying loved one by simply being present to what is; releasing our need to control the outcome; being mindful, understanding, and aware; and offering our love and support.

The greatest closure and healing for those left behind comes when they feel they have supported their loved one's good death. The person dying has shared their wishes in advance, and surviving family and friends help facilitate those wishes. It is as simple as allowing the loved one to transition painlessly, in peace and comfort.

Supporting our dying loved ones can include singing to them, talking about how much we love them, playing music, or burning incense or candles. It can comprise saying prayers or filling their space with family photos or favorite items. It can include opening a window, bringing in a pet for a visit, or doing anything that is of caring, compassionate service, even if the dying person is unresponsive.

It is important to remember we can care for a loved one during their dying days from afar. Sometimes, family and friends cannot be at the bedside of a loved one who is dying. Setting up a vigil, even at a distance, aids in the process, and on a Soul level, the dying person is aware of the added love and support. In my bedside experiences, consciousness appears to be non-local, so it stands to reason that a dying person will receive love sent from the heart despite distance or time.

The first step in holding a vigil (in person or long distance) is finding a quiet place to sit. With your eyes closed, take a few deep breaths, focusing your attention on your breath. Relax. Find peace and centeredness within you. Imagine a happy or exciting moment in your loved one's life. Maybe you simply focus on their smile or laugh. As you do so, you will feel a connection to them. Tune in to their energy and remember their joy. Now, smile with them and tap into the love you feel for them. Feel it as it ripples out in the field around you. This love is genuine. It is sent to your loved one

instantly and is eternal. This is such a simple exercise, but it has profound, lasting effects.

Many species on our beautiful planet help those among them who are dying. It is a natural part of life. It reminds us of our basic connection to one another and nature itself. One example of a species that honors their dying is the mighty elephant. Researchers have observed elephants stroking dying members of their herd with their trunks. They toss dust and place branches on and around sick and dying elephants, guard them, and take turns protecting them throughout the process. They grieve their loss as well.

Another less obvious example is the tiny ant. Ants recognize other sick ants within the colony through a change in their chemical smell. Colony members take turns licking the sick ant to remove toxins or fungi and support health. If a sick ant dies, other ants remove its dead body and place it in an ant cemetery (known as a "midden"), where they store the bodies of dead ants—they even space them evenly apart.

It is not only animals that support their communities in the dying process. Fungi have symbiotic relationships with a variety of organisms, too. Fungi break down decaying matter, releasing oxygen, nitrogen, carbon, and phosphorus into the soil, which stimulates life and growth in surrounding plants. They construct a thin web of filaments (called hyphae) under the soil, which they use to send electrical impulses to communicate with other fungi and other organisms. They exchange nutrients with trees, provide shelter for algae, and supply extra water to host forest plants in exchange for carbohydrates. Fungi are living, sensing, complex organisms that support life and death in their own colonies and in the communities of other plants and trees.

So, as you can see, species across our planet aid and support each other. It is part of our nature. None of us are separate. When we care for each other and serve one another, we all benefit. We are stronger together. Helping those in need softens our rough edges, teaches us compassion and understanding, and gives us a greater sense of self. It helps reinforce that, as beings of the Earth, we can fill individual roles and support the whole.

You are Nature. You are a part of the land, just as it is a part of you. There is no separation. For as you are creating, so is Nature, simultaneously. You are one and the same. You consciously create and express Love, joy, and purpose in distinct but connected ways. How can Man make wise decisions concerning Nature if Man identifies himself as separate from Nature? Where is the heart connection? Without it, one will continue to feel separate from All That Is, one's true nature. Remember who you truly are. There is no superiority, only harmony, and Love here.

~ A-Team

Chapter 9

Mrs. Wilma

O ne evening, I received word that NODA needed a companion for a patient who was dying in a local hospital. I signed up for a three-hour shift the following morning. Mrs. Wilma was dying alone because her family, who lived in another state, could not make the costly trip to be by her side.

Upon arriving at the facility, I located the information sheet about my patient. Mrs. Wilma was an elderly Christian Black woman who loved hymns. She had progressed in the dying process to where she was unconscious and breathing laboriously. I set up a bedside vigil: flameless tea light candles dispersed along a window ledge and gospel music playing on my speaker. I sat down to the right of Mrs. Wilma and held her hand. I started with a brief inward reflection and prayer, connecting to God, All That Is, the Unity that binds us together. I was feeling peaceful when, out of the corner of my eye, I saw a young girl walking toward me, smiling. Although I knew she was not physical, she appeared to be. She was wearing a white dress and socks with black dress shoes, her hair twisted in pigtails. She gave me the impression she was from the 1940s. I had an overwhelming sense of awareness of segregation. This was Mrs. Wilma presenting herself as a child of ten, maybe twelve years of age.

I knew I was sitting in a hospital room, holding Mrs. Wilma's hand, while communicating telepathically with a young, spiritual aspect of Mrs. Wilma. I had an awe-inspiring feeling of expansiveness, freedom, and wholeness, and a sense of knowing a profound truth. Young Mrs. Wilma said she wanted to show me something. She took my free hand and transported us to a vast forest of tall trees. Their trunks were bare, and their dense canopy soared far overhead. They sparkled and shimmered with bright, dappled light, and their shades of green were more beautiful than anything I had ever seen. The trees glowed from within, emanating light. I was acutely aware of the Life these trees embodied. I could feel them—the forest felt more alive and real than the hospital room. Young Mrs. Wilma communicated without words that we would climb the tree we were standing beside. There were no lower branches to cling to, but we glided upward swiftly to the tippy-top. When we emerged from the canopy, I was facing one direction, but could see all the way around me in a 360-degree circle without turning my head. The sky was a soft blue and was lit brightly, and the trees hummed a sound, a tone unlike anything we have here on Earth. More trees stood in all directions, as far as the eye could see.

Young Mrs. Wilma wanted to express to me the importance of being part of a greater whole, a true unity. "This one tree is as vital as that one," she said, "or that one, but each tree is minuscule compared to the greatness of the whole. Each tree has a life of its own. It has roots, each growing and dividing, seeking nourishment to help sustain something greater than itself, but it is not separate. It has branches. Each branch is a passageway that carries the water gathered from the roots in the soil to the leaves, allowing them to grow to their fullest. Branches move the food the leaves create throughout the tree, and the branches grow in individual directions. Still, they are not separate. There is a connection. The tree also has leaves. Each leaf has its own life, performing a service to feed and maintain the overall life of the tree. One tree is an entire lifeform teeming with other lifeforms, and all of them support each other. This one tree appears separate, but it is not separate from the forest. The trees in the forest connect to one another through their roots underground, creating a network of communication and nourishment. Every Life is connected. And so are we."

This was important for Young Mrs. Wilma to share, and I think it played into her lifetime of feeling separated, through segregation in her childhood, and now being separated from her family and dying alone. This must have been a vital lesson for her because I felt a knowing that this was an overarching theme in her physical life. I am grateful she chose to share her experience with me. It was profound and taught me even more about our Soul's journey during and after our physical death.

As I sat and held the elder Mrs. Wilma's hand, she struggled to breathe. It appeared she was suffering, but the forest experience juxtaposed what I was observing physically. Mrs. Wilma was fine. She was better than fine. She was free and filled with understanding, expansiveness, love, and gratitude. Her body may have been going through its natural process of shutting down, but she was okay. She was not suffering. It felt natural, as though she were shifting her awareness and focus from one reality to the next. Mrs. Wilma was learning and growing and teaching through the last part of her physical experience. As the Elder Mrs. Wilma transitioned, I was there holding her hand, and Young Mrs. Wilma was holding mine.

I love Mrs. Wilma's story because it taught me that what we perceive with our physical eyes is not always our reality. And of course, it was a beautiful reminder that we are all connected, even when we feel separate.

In one of my meditations, A-Team came through with some wisdom on unity. The awareness of the beauty of life interwoven through all other aspects of our world is a gift. Spirit explained that because I am One with myself, I am as much my spiritual Self as I am my physical self. Just as I cannot separate being a mom from being a daughter, a friend, a sister, or an aunt, I am all equally One. My physical self cannot be disconnected from my spiritual Self and I cannot be apart from All That Is. I do not need to gain access to my Higher Self or my Soul Self to feel whole. I already am. There is no difference, no separation. I am.

Truly, are you not amazed by the life teeming all around you / us? It is a wondrous thing. The dance, the symphony, the harmony, the interplay of every life interacting and supporting every other life.

Yes, wondrous. The connection that bonds, the tie that binds, can never be severed, for we are all One. One with Nature, you always have been; there can be no other way. Recognizing and respecting a life seemingly smaller than yours would be a thoughtful shift in perspective, so you could see life in your world from new points of view. This is gaining a greater understanding of Nature of which you are already One.

~ A-Team

Chapter 10

Simple Signs

As I explored the gifts of connecting outside my physical reality, I researched others who were doing the same. I took courses on spirituality, astrology, mediumship, and trance. I emailed professionals in the field, asked questions, and sat for readings. I had a relationship with Spirit already, but I wanted to improve it and use the connection better. Perhaps, I thought, if I could strengthen my relationship with Spirit, they could guide me to serve those who need a little reminder that we are eternal, loved, and never alone.

While teachings from others offered new perspectives and diverse ways of connecting to Spirit, I found I had to pick from the various teachings to explore different ways of connecting on my own. It became apparent to me that each of our journeys is unique. What works for one may not work for another. Being open and trying out new exercises and modes of connecting is helpful in discovering what works best for you.

In one online workshop, a respected medium taught us to sit and ask our guides for a physical sign, so we will feel confident we are ready to receive messages from Spirit. The idea of asking for a sign intrigued me. So, one morning I meditated and connected with a member of my Spirit team who would guide me through a mediumship practice. "Am I on the right path to explore mediumship and to interpret messages from the other side?" I asked. "If so, I'm going to need a sign... a big one. Not just a little feather... the whole freaking bird." A few minutes later, I was heading to my car in the driveway, and a homing pigeon (a.k.a. a *messenger* pigeon) flew off my roof and at my face. I saw it coming at me in slow motion. I screamed and ducked. It landed at my feet. I have never seen a pigeon in my suburban neighborhood in over fifteen years. He had bands on his legs, and later, I looked up on the internet the information stamped on the bands. He was a racing pigeon on his way home. I guess my house had been a pit stop. I was so caught up in how cool it was to be close to that bird it took me twelve hours to get the point—my team had sent me the "whole freaking bird." Message received.

As I mentioned, when I connect with A-Team for guidance, I sit where no one will disturb me. I center myself and inhale and exhale slowly. Sometimes, I imagine myself in my "Happy Place," a forest with shining shafts of light dappling a lush forest floor. There is a small stream trickling nearby. I explain to my team, out loud or quietly, what I hope to get guidance about. Then I wait and listen for a response. Sometimes I receive a message right away. At other times I perceive nothing and need to revisit the situation later with Spirit. When I do receive a response, I ask for a sign to validate my understanding of their message, and I let my guides pick what the sign will be. I say, "If I am interpreting your response correctly, I need a sign. The sign I will receive in the next couple of days, if not sooner, is...." And then I wait. An image comes to mind, and I journal it. So simple.

Signs I have received include birds, feathers, flowers, names, or even a combination of words like "happy goat." These signs are subtle but straightforward. They are not big, glowing, striking, or unusual moments outside nature's flow. That is the simple truth and beauty of it. I do not expect to see a purple monkey playing a piano in my closet. For example, perhaps I ask for a sign and see a red rose in my mind's eye. Later, while going through a drive-through for lunch, my cashier has a red rose tattoo on her arm or maybe a name tag that says, "Rose." Or perhaps I see an image of a hawk in my mind's eye, and while running my errands, I notice a hawk or two or three along my route.

Many people brush these little signs off as coincidence because they are just a part of life's flow—after all, pigeons do sometimes land at people's feet, and we often see hawks flying in the sky. Still, when you acknowledge that Spirit knew you would encounter these events later, they drop that symbol in as a sign to validate that you have interpreted their message correctly. Acknowledging these little gifts of awareness opens the floodgates for Spirit to communicate.

We can receive signs through sound, too. Sometimes, for example, Spirit sends me songs in my head as signs. Later, when that song plays in my car or over a speaker when I am at the grocery store or in a restaurant, I know that is my validation.

Once I contemplated attending a workshop by a well-respected medium in Virginia. I was in Texas, and it was a commitment for time and finances. I checked a map and realized the Blue Ridge Mountains were not too far from where the event was being held. I have always wanted to travel to that part of the country and thought, *How cool would it be to drive the Blue Ridge Parkway?* I have suggested it for vacations, and it is always a "No" from my family. *Can I swing the trip? Can I leave while the kids are in school?* It felt a little selfish to take a trip just for me. I asked Spirit, "Should I sign up for the class, rent a car, and drive the Blue Ridge Parkway? Will I gain information that will be worth it? I need a sign, as usual, a big one, please!" I finished praying and headed off to meet a client at her home.

Two hours after my request to A-Team, I got rear-ended in our fairly new ranch truck in a minor fender-bender. I had stopped, as had the driver of the vehicle behind me. But she accidentally stepped on the gas and rolled into me. My bumper sustained a scratch or two, but nothing too terrible. I snapped a picture of her ID and insurance card. Her address was 411 East Blue Ridge Parkway. "411" means information, so I took it as a sign. I was so excited! I shared what had happened with Taylor, thrilled about the synchronicity, only to have him get upset over the scratches on the truck. He did not see the value in the sign. (As an added gift from the Universe, the insurance check ended up covering the cost of my trip. Thank you, Spirit.)

What happens if I ask for a sign and receive an image but Spirit never validates it? This is common, and when it happens, I revisit Spirit and hash it out. I explain we must have had a breakdown in communication, and that I will do my part to focus more if they will do their part to "come in" more clearly. We are a team, and they are here for me, but they tell me I am here for them as well. I know they are doing their best, and I must try my best, too. I am not here to serve Spirit solely, and they are not serving me solely. But we are serving each other Soul-ly.

We are all multifaceted and are working together to serve a greater whole and ourselves. Sometimes I find myself distracted in my physical world, and I feel like I am not carrying my fair share of responsibility with my Spirit team. But they assure me I am doing just fine just as I am. But, they add, lightheartedly, "If you want to commit more time to tuning in, that will be fine, too."

> *When you are at ease, balanced, and open, you are more acutely aware of choices you might have otherwise missed if you were solely focused instead of Soul-ly focused.*
> *~ A-Team*

Chapter 11

Ms. Mildred

One day, while driving through my neighborhood to make a client house call, I noticed that a Yaupon Holly bush I pass several times a day had sprung a couple of straggly branches that resembled a cross. By most accounts, it is an unremarkable bush—but at the moment I saw it, a shaft of light hit the bush, illuminating the cross-formed branches. Instead of thinking that the bush needed to be trimmed, I had an inner knowing that the cross would be significant during my time with my client, Ms. Mildred.

As I drove to see Ms. Mildred for the first time, I felt the weight and speed of Spirit around me. When Spirit steps into my awareness, the air in my vicinity feels faster—not like wind, but an unseen energy that moves at a quicker rate than the molecules in my body. As my body responds to the faster-moving energy, I get flushed and hot, though not enough to break a sweat. I welcome the blending of my energy with that of Spirit and the process brings me peace, because I know Spirit will deliver a message and offer my client peace and an opportunity for self-healing.

Starting our meeting excited me. Ms. Mildred invited me in and offered me a seat. I sat in a soft blue velvet chair near a window while she settled in on her couch.

"Could you tune in to Spirit and see what they have to say, to shed light on what I'm going through?" She was vague, but hopeful, looking for validation and guidance.

I trusted that A-Team would help me translate the wisdom Ms. Mildred needed to bring light to her uncertainty. I felt Spirit close and expected to hear from one of her loved ones. Instead, an unexpected personality, Jesus, presented himself. As with other Spirit encounters, I saw him in my mind's eye, and was as much aware of him as I was of sitting with Ms. Mildred in her living room. Jesus sat next to her on the couch wearing an untucked white t-shirt and jeans. He had brown eyes with flecks of orangish gold, and had pulled his brown hair into a low ponytail. He gave me the overwhelming sensation that he was her equal, best friend, brother, or partner. I hesitated to share what I was seeing, second-guessing myself. *What if she's not Christian? What if she doesn't feel a connection to Jesus? Why Jesus? Am I imagining him?* Then, in my head, I heard the word "Trust." I took a deep breath, exhaled, and explained what I was seeing and feeling.

Ms. Mildred sat quietly. I felt other personalities around me, but I could not see them in the same way I was perceiving Jesus. The words I was interpreting seem to come from a larger collective consciousness, even though they appeared to come from Jesus.

Jesus told Ms. Mildred she was loved, that she is forgiven because there is nothing to forgive, and that she would benefit from showing love and forgiveness to herself. "You can be an energetic barrier or an energetic doorway, depending on your projected thoughts," he said. "Other people respond consciously and subconsciously to you based on your actions and your projected thought patterns. You respond to others and their thoughts and react accordingly."

Jesus encouraged Ms. Mildred to notice her thoughts and to think in a manner conducive to the positive life she wants for herself. "Changing thought patterns is easy," he said, "as it requires a simple conscious awareness of a greater whole and an empathetic understanding that we are all growing and learning from all our choices. Just because our physical eyes do not perceive something does not mean it is not there. The same accounts for thoughts and the energy and intent behind them." Jesus expressed the benefits for Ms. Mildred of removing her negative inner thought patterns, her self-sabotaging beliefs, and her fear of others' judgment. Other personal details followed, but his overall message was one of love and compassion for Self.

As the information I perceived faded, I waited for Ms. Mildred's reaction. She explained she used to be a Chaplain in a local hospital. She had used the brotherly teachings of Jesus to aid in dying patients' transitions and had sought biblical quotes from his teachings. She found solace in his words and felt a deep connection with him. On her left hand, she wore a ring she told me later signified her devotion to him and symbolized her marriage of the heart to Jesus. She told me she had hung an image of him in her bedroom so he would be the first person she saw when she woke up in the morning and the last person she saw before going to sleep at night. She was a devoted, loving companion to Jesus and his teachings were inspiring to her. As devout as she was, there were no symbols or altars in her living room that denoted her religious beliefs.

While contemplating Jesus's messages, Ms. Mildred recognized correlations from her childhood that contributed to her limiting beliefs about herself. She shared details of her upbringing and what she believed to be the root of her painful thoughts and self-judgment. Jesus's message resonated with her, and she needed time to process everything that had come through. She had not realized how much she had misunderstood—how her choices sprang from feelings of lack and fear, or how she created problems through beliefs about herself and others. Ms. Mildred analyzed her experiences and recognized that based on her beliefs, she had done the best she could with the tools and resources she had. In hindsight, she might have chosen differently, she said, but she had done what she thought was best. Now, she could embrace herself in a more compassionate, forgiving, and understanding light.

You have caused hurt and pain and brought joy, Love, light, and strength. Love yourself. You are worthy. Do not collect others' perceived feelings and emotions into a cistern to stagnate. Release them. Now is all there is. Forgive others, they say... I say, forgive yourself. Forgive yourself. Forgive yourself. You are Love, and you are loved.
~ *A-Team*

Chapter 12

Forgiveness and Fear

Two issues that often arise on the deathbed of dying people are forgiveness and fear. People who are dying can feel fearful or ensnared by feelings of guilt, remorse, or resentment about past situations that require forgiveness of the self, or others. Being bound to this physical world by fear—of death, the unknown, or anything, really—can interrupt the peaceful flow of our physical death. It is important to resolve issues of fear and (un)forgiveness so we can free ourselves from the human sentiments that keep us shackled to this world.

Unforgiveness and fear teach us to recognize our humanity and our authenticity. But hanging on to fear and (un)forgiveness are choices we make. Both choices are charged emotionally, especially for those who have experienced trauma. Trauma survivors can feel helpless and victimized, sometimes for their entire lives. The answer to this life-denying dilemma? *Forgiveness*.

Forgiveness is a loaded word, and those who have experienced life-altering trauma at the hands of another person can find the idea of forgiveness offensive. Often, survivors of trauma or abuse have a hard time accepting (or even uttering) the word "forgiveness" because they do not want to excuse the offender's behavior. They do not align with the word.

We can, however, reframe the word *forgiving*. Words such as *releasing, unburdening*, or *unloading* are sufficient. Forgiveness is a way for people to free themselves from the power their past trauma holds over them. This means releasing the grip trauma has on one's self-identity, and freeing oneself from the misery the trauma has fostered. Forgiving, releasing, and unburdening means letting go of hurt, anger, resentment, injustice, and the desire for retribution toward those who have wronged you. Forgiving someone is not excusing or forgetting any action, but is a conscious, deliberate choice to let go. As the saying goes, forgiveness is not for the other person. Forgiveness is for *you*.

It takes effort to carry inner turmoil around. Freeing yourself from the heavy burden of trauma and other people's wrongs creates space for positive, uplifting experiences, such as inspiration, joy, and love for yourself and others to come into your life. It ushers in a greater sense of compassion and empathy, which helps you better understand humanity and those around you. After all, we are all entangled, connected, and one.

Forgiveness takes time. Everyone processes their emotions differently. One way to facilitate this release is to find someone you trust who will listen to your story, and who will allow you to speak out loud about your emotions and thoughts without judgment for as long as you need. Your listener does not need to offer you advice. Many people with good intentions offer advice based on what they would do in someone else's situation to help or fix a problem. But advice does not always sink in as well as the self-realization that can come from processing one's own experience. So, the person you choose as your listener needs to sit and listen with their full attention and respect. A good listener waits for you to come to resolutions and conclusions on your own. There does not need to be fixing or forcing.

Venting and letting loose pent-up feelings is both lightening and enlightening. When people express themselves in a safe space, allowing the openness and vulnerability of being their unadulterated selves, they can process their feelings and experience revelations. A person releasing trauma may need to go through this process only once or many times—regardless, healing occurs.

As the healing process unfolds, the doorway to forgiveness and letting go opens and you experience insights and alternative actions for future challenges. You release stagnant, repetitive patterns and embrace strength and self-worth. You no longer identify as a victim, and you let go of expectations for how things should have been (or are supposed to be). When you accept things as they are, you understand your own value in the world, improve your quality of life, and free yourself from the limiting thought of (un)forgiveness. You see the world through a new lens. This fresh worldview instills in you the desire to help others see their own worthiness as well. Forgiveness is a compassionate action with a far-reaching ripple effect!

As noted, the other side of the forgiveness-and-fear paradigm is fear. Fear is an awareness of danger or a reticence to experience an unwanted physical or emotional experience. Fear can be real or imagined. Often, we fear a future event that may or may not happen, and usually, our fear focuses on worse-case outcomes. Fear can stifle our creativity, divert our focus from tasks at hand, and distract our attention from achieving our goals. A-Team once said:

> Judgment, hate, and fear can blind some people. Forgiveness and understanding are the path to true freedom; Love follows, for where there is Love, there is light, and light will illuminate the world for those blinded by their own perceived darkness. Remove your thumbs from the weighted scales of humanity and seek balance and truth.

On the positive side, fear is also vital to our survival on this planet. It allows us to respond to impending danger instinctively and remain alert for our own protection. Some people believe fear is a positive, motivating factor in progress and performance because it can help a person achieve desired outcomes. Without fear, they say, we would end up in predictable situations, leaving us inattentive and depressed.

Fear starts in our heads, in the amygdala. The amygdala is a part of the limbic system (which means "edge" because the amygdala is at the base of the brain). However, if subjected to prolonged anxiety, the amygdala can leave us feeling on edge. Once your brain decides you are in danger, the amygdala signals the hypothalamus, which activates your pituitary gland, which triggers your adrenal gland to release a barrage of hormones, including adrenaline and cortisol, to prepare for a response to a threat.

Our amygdala attaches emotions to our memories. This can make our memories seem more traumatic (or more enjoyable) as we recall them. Such memories may be real or they may be irrational fears. Irrational fears limit us, keeping us from embracing beautiful moments and experiencing life to the fullest. Letting go of irrational fears allows us to express ourselves fully in love, creativity, joy, and gratitude.

Our sense of fear can infringe on all our normal emotional states. In this sense, fear is negative, because it can stop us from coping with life's risks and dangers. For example, those who have experienced past traumas can get locked into imagining undesired possibilities around every corner and live in perpetual anxiety.

Anxiety differs from fear. It is a persistent feeling of being in harm's way or a feeling that life is overwhelming. Many of us push past our worries, but sometimes anxiety can crush us. Anxiety can feel physical. We can become short of breath (because we breathe faster), our blood pressure goes up, we get flushed, and we get tunnel vision. Our blood diverts to our muscles and away from our digestive tract, to help us prepare for the extra strength we'll need to flee from danger. This, of course, makes us not want to eat or drink. Our body can feel like it is burning, and our limbs can feel numb. This response can be scary, creating more fear, and then the body bombards us with hormones, creating a challenging cycle that is difficult to overcome. These physical reactions are all part of the fight-or-flight response. How can we combat this?

One way we can pull ourselves out of the fight-or-flight response is to fight—not another person, but we can punch a punching bag or pillow to complete the response. Another strategy is flight. We can go for a brisk walk, go for a run, or do jumping jacks. This physical activity helps the body process chemicals and settle down. We also can practice mindfulness. We can ask ourselves, "How did the conversation or thoughts that occurred just before my panic set in affect me?" Once we are aware of those thoughts, we can understand why we responded the way we did, and we can assess how to manage such a response in the future.

Forgiveness and fear are both vital aspects of our life experience on earth. Choosing how we want to go through life affects the outcomes we create for ourselves. Spirit once advised one of my clients:

> *Do not fear. Release the emotional knots that tie you to your childhood traumas. You cling to these challenges to give your feelings of fear a voice. All experiences make you who you are NOW. Untether yourself with gratitude for what was and honor what is; this is where your power lies. Emotional insecurities and fear-based emotions tie you to your past. Right now, you are safe. Let go of what was and what could be and focus on the present you. You are never alone. You are supported in all you choose to manifest, but we encourage you to let go of the past sufferings. They will drag you down, adding weight to your emotional baggage. Let go of what no longer serves you. You will be provided for; you always have been. You are loved.*

This message applies to all of us. It reminds us to release and unburden ourselves from our past and to forgive. It encourages us to seek our peace in the present moment. These are choices we make consciously. Spirit reminds us we are safe and provided for and that we are never alone. Addressing our fears is hard work and while it is challenging, we emerge feeling free, and experiencing harmony within. Embracing open-hearted forgiveness of ourselves and others also calms internal turmoil and brings us lasting peace. I love how simple a truth this is. With mindfulness, we can shift our thoughts to change our view of life.

What you create is up to you. Disappointment, fear, anger, and guilt are all choices. Happiness, love, acceptance, and understanding are all choices, too. What do you choose? May we suggest lifting the hearts around you in happiness, love, acceptance, and understanding, and offer them grace instead of justifying their choices of hurt or pain. Teach another path.

~ A-Team

Chapter 13

Sister Bernadette

Sister Bernadette was a Catholic nun, and a strict, dedicated, and diligent follower of the guidelines of her faith. She heard God's calling to join her order, the Sisters of Charity of the Incarnate Word, in early adulthood, and worked as a nurse in a local Christian hospital for most of her life. She served her community by offering religious counseling to patients and assisting other nurses with their daily rounds. After decades of supporting many patients through their dying process, Sister Bernadette found herself in need of the same support.

I first met Sister Bernadette in the fall, during a time of unseasonably cool temperatures. She was sitting up in her bed holding a rosary in silent prayer. As I entered her room, I cleared my throat to let her know I was there. She opened her eyes, smiled, and greeted me. She reached out her hands. I took them in mine, and she invited me to sit down with her. The nursing staff had informed me that Sister Bernadette was declining, so her lucidity and warm, welcoming demeanor surprised me. She was a gracious hostess, and I felt comfortable in her space.

After introductions and formalities, Sister Bernadette discussed her diagnosis and her prognosis with sterile, matter-of-fact clarity. After a moment of silence, she glanced out her window and told me she saw a squirrel race across the parking lot and run up an old oak tree. She launched into a story from her childhood about a baby squirrel that had fallen from its nest. Her family took mercy on the poor animal and nursed it back to health. They named her Eve, and she became a beloved family pet. Saving that squirrel was the first time Sister Bernadette had cared for one of God's creatures and she recognized she wanted to do that forever. She loved serving the sick and less fortunate. It gave her purpose and a sense of fulfillment to know God was witnessing her deeds, and she believed it was her duty to serve Him above all else.

I listened to my new friend reminisce about her life's work. When our visit ended, I said goodbye and promised to visit later in the week. She sent me off with a smile and a sense of ease.

At each visit, Sister Bernadette shared stories from her childhood. Many involved the care of animals and the hardships of growing up in poverty. She prayed to St. Francis, the patron saint of animals, and teared up when she told me stories of animals enduring pain or injustice. Her stories were repetitive, but each time she repeated a story, I listened as enthusiastically as I had the first time.

Weeks after our initial visit, Sister Bernadette had a setback with her health that shifted her perspective. The next time I met with her, she did not tell me childhood stories. Instead, she announced she had a confession to make, but that she would appreciate my time and undivided attention. She did not want a priest.

I sat and listened.

Sister Bernadette told me she was afraid of dying. She had counseled many patients about sin, hell, and forgiveness, she said, but for herself, she feared God would judge her. She did not believe she would go to hell, but she knew that in her heart she had condemned others for what she deemed immoral or wrong behavior. She compared everyone to the impossible and limiting (albeit holy) guidelines her faith required. While she knew there were inconsistencies in her teachings and beliefs, the overall beauty and goodness of her religious convictions offered her a firm foundation and set of rules by which to live. Would God judge her for judging others? She hoped He would understand and see that she had tried her best to uphold His word. But would He be as strict with her as she'd been with others? "What do you think?" she asked.

"I think the way you feel is normal," I said. "Everyone questions themselves before significant transitions, decisions, and opportunities. You did the best you could in every moment. We all do, and when we look back and realize we fell short, we try again. That's part of our journey here, our own Soul's growth. If you're recognizing your own shortcomings, that's a good thing, and it shows you are learning. That's being human, and if God is as understanding as you believe He is, everything will be fine. If God's judgment is part of your faith, why fear it? If it doesn't happen, there is nothing to fear. If it does, then everyone has to go through it. Don't think of it as judgment, but more like a review. Your life is filled with beautiful, compassionate, holy deeds, and God will consider those, too."

Sister Bernadette sighed. She thought about my words and said she needed time to contemplate our discussion. I told her I would see her next week.

Less than five days had passed when I stopped in to check on Sister Bernadette. She seemed more stoic than usual. When I walked in, she said, "I want to make another confession."

"Do you want me to call the priest?"

She declined. Like last week, she wanted me to listen. She asked me not to judge her and told me that another Sister from her convent was visiting her.

I smiled. "That's nice."

"No," she said. "You don't understand. Sister Mary Catherine has already died and joined our heavenly Father, and yet she is here with me right now and has been for days."

"How does that make you feel?"

Sister Bernadette declared that seeing her old friend brought her peace. "I know she is as real as we are, but my faith restricts me from communing with her, from communing with the dead."

I smiled. "You talk to the dead all the time," I reminded her. "Including Jesus, Mother Mary, and many saints."

"No. I pray to the dead but I don't talk to them."

"What does Sister Mary Catherine say?"

"Sister Mary Catherine tells me we'll take a trip soon."

"That's an exciting offer. Where are you going?"

"I'm not sure."

We sat for a few minutes, processing the gravity of her confession. To comfort her, I told her that many people see loved ones as their time draws near. I scolded myself silently for having suggested that her time was drawing near, and to smooth it over, I added that Catholic saints and figures throughout history talked to God, questioned Him, received visits from angels, and had visions. Perhaps Sister Mary Catherine was a vision and her presence was divine, not sinful.

Sister Bernadette smiled weakly and said, "Bless you, child. I like the sound of that." She closed her eyes and drifted off to sleep.

The following day, I received a call asking me to visit Sister Bernadette if I had time. I stopped in to see my new friend and realized she was well into the actively dying phase. I remained by her side as many nurses, doctors, and other hospital staff stopped in to say their goodbyes. It was clear she was a well-respected and cared-for woman. Her service to her community did not go unnoticed, and the love that poured into her room that day was palpable. Sister Bernadette felt the love and gratitude, and it started a beautiful and peaceful transition. She passed away as friends and loved ones congregated and paid their respects to a woman who served their community devoutly. I am sure Sister Mary Catherine was waiting eagerly to accompany Sister Bernadette on their trip.

Dwelling on the actions of others can stifle your understanding of the world in which you live. Assuming another may have a more difficult path or has somehow failed to rise up spiritually is a judgment passed. There is only now. One's actions are but a stepping stone to their own growth goals. They are not less than or worse off in any way. They are becoming, just as you are.
~ A-Team

Chapter 14

Anxiety and Anger About Death

"I don't think I can do this." "I'm scared." "What's going to happen to me?" "It wasn't supposed to be like this." "This isn't fair." "I'm not ready!" These are all phrases I hear while sitting beside dying patients. Panic, anxiety, and anger are common responses to processing one's unavoidable death, both for the patient and their surviving loved ones.

Facing what many consider the biggest challenge of their lives—often before they are ready and when they are at their weakest—leads many people to spiral into fearful thoughts. Discomfort, restlessness, or feeling "out-of-control" forces many dying people to resist their current state. This increases their anxiety. Often, panic attacks arise, which can feel life-threatening. When a patient experiences waves of panic, it can scare them even more. They think their time to die has arrived, and they succumb to a cycle of fear and resistance. Then, when a family member reacts to the dying person's fear and spirals into anxiety and panic themselves, everyone's attention moves away from the dying patient to support the family member in crisis. This reinforces the patient's feelings of helplessness, hopelessness, and fear.

Many caregivers choose to medicate patients who feel fearful, and while this can be helpful, reminding those who are dying and their families to be mindful of their thoughts is a good support strategy. Caregivers can start by discussing the dying process, so the patient and their family know what to expect. In this way, they are not caught off guard, and they are less likely to feel fearful or anxious. Discussing beliefs about the afterlife and sharing stories of near-death experiences can ease fear and bring hope. If the family and patient are open to less conventional thought, I have found that discussing the evidence mediums offer about the Spirit world can be comforting for both patients and their loved ones.

It is not always possible to help a dying person avoid having a panic attack. And, for those observing their loved one suffering through a full-blown panic attack (that can last for hours), it is difficult. They feel helpless. The best strategy is to sit with the person going through the episode, and to hold their hand or touch them so they feel connected and not alone. You can talk softly about positive things, remind them to breathe slowly, and reassure them they are safe. Letting them know you are present, protecting them, and ready to get further help if needed takes away a bit of their fear. It helps to let them know what their brain is doing (see section on the amygdala, above) and how their body is reacting, so there is a medical understanding of their experience. There is not always a way to stop this, but some medicines can help. Surrendering to the experience and reminding them they are safe is the best option when medicines are not readily available.

There are many suggestions, techniques, and tools that can help ease a dying person's (or their loved ones') stress and anxiety and create peace. These include:

- Try box breathing. Inhale for four seconds, hold your breath for four seconds, exhale for four seconds, and hold your breath once more for four seconds.
- Practice slow breathing, exhaling longer than you inhale.
- Do a body scan. Focus on different areas of your body, being conscious of any pain or tension, and relaxing each muscle to ease the stress.
- Practice guided imagery.
- Try repetitive chanting.
- Pray.

Going through the dying process with a loved one is a high-stress, emotional time. Fear and anxiety can dominate a dying person's bedside space, but family members can also feel angry at the dying patient or at other family members. The patient can direct anger at caregivers and even at God. Often, a sense of loss of control and unresolved feelings of hurt and pain can accompany the anger.

Anger can appear when we do not feel safe or when we feel helpless. Loved ones and patients can repeat phrases like, "Why me?" "It's not supposed to be this way," or "I don't deserve this." The dying person may feel they are being punished for their life actions or choices. Those holding vigil at a dying person's bedside may even feel angry wondering why their good and loving family member has to die when the world is full of "bad" people.

Often, we express our anger not in words, but through our bodies and in our minds. We may tense up and think about saying hurtful words or doing unkind things. Our thoughts can loop as we blame, justify, or fear the inevitable outcome of death. We can feel a need to purge our pent-up energies and may lash out at others, shouting, hitting, or throwing things to ease our anger. A-Team once shared, "To think and rethink of the painful experience brought on by the words of another only causes suffering within you. They are just words, said once. Do not continue to rehash them, because you are only hurting yourself. Think loving thoughts and send love out."

Taking time each day for a little self-care to deal with your anger can be helpful. First, you can stop and examine whether your feelings of resentment or anger are a way of coping with other underlying emotions such as fear. Are you afraid of abandonment? Do you feel lonely or helpless? If fear is the underlying component, taking steps to ease your fear can be helpful in releasing your anger. Support groups and counselors are excellent sources of information to help personalize your healing journey. Listening to others speak about how they dealt with their emotions after a similar experience can be helpful.

Another important way of dealing with pent-up anger is to express it healthily. Screaming into a pillow (outside away from others, in your car, or in the bathroom) is a good way of releasing stifled emotions. Exercising, boxing, running, and yoga are just a few physical activities that can ease anger. Sometimes, if we feel weak emotionally, taking part in fitness activities can empower us and make us feel strong physically.

Talking to our loved ones, even if they are deceased, has a way of bringing peace and solace and allows us to express ourselves without fear of judgment. Whether we are the family member who will be left behind or the one who is dying, speaking freely with loved ones helps us feel heard and affords us a clearer mindset in which to process our grief. Sharing our deepest feelings can usher in a new level of acceptance and awareness.

Feeling anxiety or anger around death is normal, and an expected part of the grieving process. When someone responds with anger, it is helpful to be understanding, but can be hard not to take personally when directed at you. Take a deep breath and let the emotions wash over you.

Not everyone who is going through grief will experience the same emotions. Not feeling anger does not mean a person is not processing grief. We all grieve in our own way and, contrary to the assertions of many therapists, counselors, and other experts, there are no set stages of grief.

As we navigate the potential for anxiety and anger around death and dying, maintaining an awareness of how our words and actions affect others will offer us grace when we need it the most. Our feelings are real and worthy of being processed in a healthy way.

Be present. Pay attention to the story. Shift perspectives and see from a new angle. Practice feeling your way with others and imagine quite literally being in their shoes, not what you think you would do but feeling what they ARE doing. What is this experience teaching you?

~ A-Team

Chapter 15

Mr. Virgil

One hot summer night, NODA asked for volunteers to sit with a dying patient at the hospital. I checked the online portal and noticed other volunteers had filled all the convenient times. Most people do not want the midnight to 3:00 a.m. shift, for example. There was an opening, however, at 6:00 a.m. It was already late. Did I want to commit to a 5:00 a.m. wake-up call? I could not shake the need to be there, so before falling asleep I told Spirit, "If it is the highest good for me to be there tomorrow, wake me up around 4:30 a.m. and I will sign up for the 6:00 a.m. shift it is still available." I did not set the alarm, and the ball was in Spirit's court. At 4:28 a.m. I woke up with the song "Colors" by the Black Pumas playing in my head.[1] "Okay, guys," I said, "I'll sign up."

I got in the car and drove to the downtown hospital before sunrise. To help myself wake up a little more, I turned on the radio. "Colors" by the Black Pumas came on, and I had an inner knowing that the NODA patient I was about to meet would be a Black man. I arrived at the hospital in time for my shift and the patient, Mr. Virgil, was indeed a Black man, in his 50s. He had severe lung disease and struggled to breathe. For four hours, I watched Mr. Virgil find thirty to ninety seconds of calm followed by an intense thirty seconds of what appeared to be panic-induced shaking, shortness of breath, sweating, and clammy skin. Nurses gave him anti-anxiety medicines, but they did not seem to stop his cycle of calm and panic.

---

[1] Black Pumas, "Colors," Black Pumas (Virgin Music, 2019), Produced by Adiran Quesada, Recorded at Deluxe Recorders in Austin.

As I settled in, I spoke to Mr. Virgil, and even though he was unresponsive, I felt his body relax a little. His overwhelming anxiety was understandable. I hoped I could help him feel grounded and supported through touch and talking. When my physical efforts did not help as much as I had intended, I turned inward, to connect and bring him peace differently.

I closed my eyes and began to connect with All That Is. Before I could devote myself in prayer, however, I was transported to another space—a beautiful place in the heart of nature. The scene laid out before me seemed to glow from within. Everything was alive, and light emanated from every life form. A vast field of bright yellow flowers swayed against a backdrop of bright blue sky. The meadow hummed with a harmonic and transcendent sound, unlike any earthly instrument. Soft, unobtrusive, and tranquil, there was no beat or rhythm and it seemed to flow through me. Off to the right was a wooded area. It was darker there but felt warm and safe. *What lies beyond it?* I wondered. As I stood there, taking in the beauty, I saw Mr. Virgil standing in the flowers, staring into the woods, as curious as I was.

Then something unexpected happened. I (or what appeared to be *me*), walked out of the woods, stood on the edge of the forest, and greeted Mr. Virgil. I was bigger than him and glowing with bluish white light. I was transparent but also solid. I was aware of myself in three places at once: I was sitting at Mr. Virgil's bedside, standing in a field of flowers, and emerging from a forest. It was new and fascinating, and I was excited to see what I might say or do.

Mr. Virgil asked the Me of Light, "Where am I?"

"I've been waiting for you," I said. "Come join me on a walk through the woods when you are ready." I could hear a celebration coming from beyond the forest and saw a flash of a party with red balloons and red roses. The woman front and center was Mr. Virgil's mom. It was a welcome home party, and it was revving up.

Mr. Virgil looked up at me. "What will happen to my body? What will happen to me? What will happen if I go?"

The Me of Light smiled and explained the physical steps of the body shutting down and remaining with the earth. "We'll go on a short walk through the forest to see your loved ones who are waiting for you," I said, sending a feeling to him that he could trust me to deliver him into the welcoming arms of his loved ones. I was overflowing with love for him, a man I had never met until now. I did not know his history, but it did not matter.

Mr. Virgil put his hands on his hips and looked down. He revealed some of his actions in life that made him feel unworthy to enter the forest—"sins" he felt were too great, and actions that were hurtful to himself and others. He was remorseful.

Still glowing in light, I presented him with a beautifully wrapped box with a purple satin ribbon. I explained he was in this box—Mr. Virgil's personality, the life he had lived, and his choices, regrets, joys, lessons, laughs, and sorrows. It was his gift of life, his gift of experiences. At any point he could open the box and remember everything life as Mr. Virgil offered. All of it was a gift, every action, every choice, even those he deemed less than ideal.

All three parts of me were engaged in the scene, independently and simultaneously. As Mr. Virgil stepped into the dark, lush forest with the Me of Light, mixed emotions overcame him. The forest transformed into a backdrop of stars, outer space, and the heavens. I became huge, much larger than I already was. I scooped Mr. Virgil into my arms like I would a child. I cradled him, rocked him, soothed him, and kissed the top of his head. As he calmed, he stood up, ready to continue our walk.

Once again, we were back in the forest, holding hands and walking to our destination. Mr. Virgil was still physical looking, and I was still the Me of Light. I knew that as we got closer to the party, he would lighten up some.

Mr. Virgil stopped me. "What will happen to my son and uncle?"

I turned to look him in the eye. Once again, I became the observer, watching the moment unfold from somewhere back near the field of flowers. The Me of Light showed him a fast flash of images of potential outcomes for both of them. They were projected to him, so the observing Me could not see or make sense of the images.

He seemed satisfied and took my glowing hand once more. As the sound of the party grew louder and the trees thinned, we began seeing the trimmings of the celebration before us. There was so much bustle, excitement, joy, and anticipation. We could see the group gathered there, and some of them were aware of our presence. We could see Mr. Virgil's mother, and her bright smiling face.

Mr. Virgil stopped me. "May I have a moment alone?" He sat on a fallen tree limb on the ground at edge of the forest.

I left his side and turned to walk back into the woods.

Just then, a nurse walked into Mr. Virgil's room sending me jolting back to a single, physical focus. She introduced herself and checked her patient's vitals. She chatted about her shift ending and her weekend plans with an upcoming bachelorette party, unaware of the beautiful moment she had interrupted. I laughed to myself, imagining her timeline of an upcoming party celebrating the end of a bachelorette life and the beginning of a married life, merging with the welcome party on Mr. Virgil's timeline, the end of a physical life and the remembering of a lighter life. Both are valid, important, and worthy of love and celebration. *How beautiful it all is.*

I stayed present with Mr. Virgil for a short time more. A new volunteer arrived to take over the next shift. Mr. Virgil did not take his last breath on my watch, but I knew he was close. I got in my car and listened to the song "Colors" again. I loved how the song described the beautiful colors of a meadow, the sky, and trees. It resonated with the welcoming scene Mr. Virgil and I had found ourselves in, somewhere between our physical reality and a lighter reality. The lyrics also refer to being accompanied to the other side. I had not noticed that before. It made me smile, because this was the first time I had walked someone to the other side.

I drove to lunch to meet a friend. I arrived a little early and waited in an enclosed patio. A short time later, a bright red cardinal pecked at the window. It was a sign. My phone whistled with a text message from NODA telling me Mr. Virgil had passed away. I thanked Spirit for the wake-up call and the chance to sit with him. I know he was celebrating with his loved ones.

Consider the pages of a book. With each new page, each new chapter, will come new challenges—ones not yet considered. These, too, will offer a richness of experiences (which you want), lessons and tests of boundaries, patience, conflict resolution, and understanding. Trust and follow your heart, not your head. You are limited only by what you place on yourself. All choices are right and will lead to varying degrees of accomplishments (from your perspective). There is no real wrong or right, only different viewpoints to the same conundrum. Be the pivot point. See all sides. Flex. Bend. There is wisdom in this. Say Yes to opportunities. We are here supporting you. Know what you believe to be your limitations and push through them, for you are limitless. We help you push through those barriers of self-imposed limitations. You are never alone. Enjoy your unfolding because unwrapping the gift is just as fun and exciting as the gift itself.

~ A-Team

Chapter 16

Judgments, Comparisons, and Truth

We are all connected. We are all One. These are simple words, but big ideas that are easier to express than to comprehend. As we go through our earthly lives, we recognize we are individuals. We appear separate in every way. Each of us experiences joy and pain at different times and processes them in unique ways. Each of us makes varying choices and has a distinct worldview.

Because we appear separate, we strive to form bonds and create communities in which we can feel a part of something bigger than ourselves. The need to be accepted and included is an innate part of the human condition. As we strive to form outside connections to other individuals, we adjust our behaviors to what we think others will accept. In doing so, often we hide or ignore the truth of who we are, how we feel, and what we want or need from others. We wonder, "What will others feel about or think of our behavior?" We project our fear of rejection onto the group, and a pattern emerges: we alter our behavior for others, question our actions, and compare ourselves to those around us, all of which keeps us from expressing ourselves authentically. We form judgments about ourselves and others to control how we hope others will perceive us. We might even want someone to change their ways to validate our set of ethics or beliefs.

A-Team reminds us:

You can't change someone, and why would you want to? Who are you to say someone needs to change? We are all equally beautiful in the eyes of God, of All That is. Believe it. Your way of living, thinking, or believing is not somehow better than anyone else's. It's all just experiences.

Judgment and comparison keep us questioning our value and that of others. In this state, we see ourselves only as physically separate individuals, rather than the greater reality of our connection: we are so much more than our bodies. Inside, we are similar. Rather than following the path of our hearts and living the lives we desire, we choose to do what we believe others will find acceptable.

Choosing to live in truth and to live fully creates opportunities for a better quality of life. Recognizing our individuality in physical form while realizing we are much more than our bodies is essential to our spiritual growth. We are all Spirit. We do not need to attain spirituality—it is already a part of us—we just need to know it. But how can we just "know it?" Do we know through judgment or discernment? There is a difference between the two. Judgment is drawing a conclusion about the character or validity of someone or something through an imposed set of ethics or morals. Discernment is the ability to use wisdom and experience to perceive and understand something, especially something that is not obvious or straightforward. But while *knowing* is beyond judgment and beyond discernment—we require both to realize the truth of who we are.

For example, often, we encounter situations that do not resonate or align with us. But just because something is not right for us does not mean it is "bad" and therefore, wrong for everyone else. Instead, it means the situation is not appropriate for us right now. That undesirable experience may be what someone else needs to experience—something from which they can learn. It is not our place to judge others. We must discern what we need to experience to remain in alignment with our truth.

Truth. It is a powerful, complex word. When seeking answers to life's biggest questions, one grapples with truth. *What is truth? What is and isn't true?* A woman may look at herself, for example, and say, "I am a mother," or "I have brown hair." While these may be accurate observations now, they have not always been so. She was not always a mother, and she may not always have had (and may not always have) brown hair. Such in-the-moment truths are ways we can define who we are, but these truths are not eternal; they are personal. A-Team said:

> *Personal truth is different for each one of you. You glow with Love, with light, and you are easy for us to see. Sometimes you dim your light, and we surround you to encourage you to turn it back up. Brighter light helps you find your way back home, back to Love, think loving thoughts do loving, kind deeds. These are not just words. They are actions. They are true. All lights dim from time to time, and we feel lost. But as they brighten again, we find our way. Love of Self is the hardest because you do not judge others as harshly as yourself. If you treated yourself with the same compassion as you do others, your light would shine for all to see. Honor your emotions. They are real for you. But then pack them up in a trunk of experiences you learn and grow from. Be grateful for every moment of exposure, happy, sad, Love, hate, fear, joy, and tears, for you got to experience that; but then proceed with Love and gratitude, for this is the way to growth. When you dwell on the pain and suffering of others brought on by their own actions and free will, you dishonor the process of the experience and that Soul's opportunity and potential to learn and grow from that struggle.*

Spiritually speaking, our truth is eternal. We are aspects of the Creator (or All That Is), and we are always becoming. As beings experiencing ourselves in physical form, we make choices and act them out. Sometimes, we regret our choices. So, we judge ourselves for our actions. But this is not truth. The truth would recognize we made those choices or expressed ourselves based on how we knew ourselves to be at that moment—including all our comparisons, fears, and hopes. Our actions are just actions, regrettable or not. They are not the truth of who we are on a Soul level. Our true Self knows that it is one with all other beings, equal in all ways.

To believe you are better than or less than another person is not living in truth. We are in a state of becoming and when we realize we can do better, we do. We get to be here, on this planet in this moment in space and time, learning, growing, and experiencing, free of eternal judgment. We want and need challenges on a Soul level. It is how we gain knowledge and grow. Life on this beautiful planet is full of experiences and challenges and we do not have all the answers. How could understanding and learning take place if we did?

Hello, young, hungry one. You question why we don't give you all the answers to questions you ask. We ask you, where's the fun in that? Your Soul knows you are safe. Your Soul loves the excitement. Your Soul craves learning/experiencing! Why would we take that away from you? You want/need challenges for your own joy, understanding, and growth. You get to choose from them like a buffet. This is something new and different! You get to go through this life choosing new experiences, sampling ideas, tasting small joys and pleasures, and devouring opportunities. But who prepared and put this spread out? Why you did, of course (a full course!) We will join in on your meal/celebration, and we, too, will enjoy it. But we won't tell you what to eat. You must try things for yourself. We might tell you about a dish, but it is always your choice to partake. Once you choose, we can guide you, offering suggestions and pairings. Thank you for inviting us. We can't wait to see what you choose next at your smorgasbord. Cheers.

~ A-Team

Chapter 17

Mr. Robinson

M r. Robinson, a patient of mine, exemplified the adage, "It's never too late." I met him in the dining hall of a nursing home as he finished lunch. He had taken only a few bites. Elderly, frail, bald, and attached to an oxygen tank, he sat in his wheelchair with his head in his hands. I introduced myself and explained I would like to visit him.

"Why?" he asked, looking at me through pained eyes. "I'm with hospice," I explained. "I visit other patients here, and I'd like to get to know you."

"All you need to know about me is that I'm in pain and I want to be alone."

"I understand," I said. "I'll leave you for now, but I'll come back to visit again in a few days."

Mr. Robinson shook his head and waved me off.

On my next visit, I found Mr. Robinson in his room. I startled him. He was not expecting me and did not make it easy for me to talk to him. If I wanted to communicate with him, I would have to follow him.

"I'm going for a stroll," he told me, and I accompanied his wheelchair through the nursing home halls.

We stopped in a lobby, and I pulled up a chair. Mr. Robinson filled the silence with small talk. He shared some of his scientific career achievements and his pride in his older brother, who had already passed on. At that moment, a gentleman in spirit appeared over his left shoulder dressed in a military uniform. I knew this to be his brother. In my experience, when loved ones who have transitioned appear behind someone who is still in the physical, I know the patient is not long for our earthly world. Loved ones who have passed show up in absolute joy, which was the case with Mr. Robinson's brother. He was beaming.

Mr. Robinson chatted about his childhood for over an hour. I listened, amused by his happiness at the recalled memories. "Why would you want to visit an old man like me, and ever want to step foot in a facility filled with dying people?" he asked. "I can't fathom why anyone would be here unless they had no choice."

"I have a choice. I do this because I love it. The last days of dying people are just as important as their first days and I hope I can bring peace and comfort to people like you."

Mr. Robinson smiled. "No, that can't be it." The scientist in him wanted a more logical answer.

"You can believe me or not. It doesn't matter. But I plan to be back next week." I stood up. "Goodbye," I said. "I'll see you soon."

"Not if I see you first," he replied. That was the first time I had glimpsed his shining, fun personality.

My third trip to visit Mr. Robinson was playful, considering the subdued nature of many of my patients. As I rounded the corner, I ran into him wheeling through the hallway. Once again, I startled him. He was on his way to a mid-morning activity, so I escorted him. The nursing staff had a weekly game of balloon volleyball set up in the lunchroom. They positioned a net across a lunch table, and wheelchair patients and a few mobile patients sitting in dining chairs gathered into two teams around each side of the net. A nurse handed a balloon to one team member, who served it across the net to the other side. The laughs and brief moments of pure joy that lit Mr. Robinson's face blew me away, as he stretched his lanky arms from the seat of his wheelchair to hit a pink balloon over the net to the opposing team. He loved this activity and took part each week. "It's one of the few things I look forward to," he said. It was an activity I looked forward to, too.

After that, our visits got easier. He still joked every time he saw me coming by. He would turn his wheelchair and go in the opposite direction or speed up as fast as he could, pretending to avoid me. Several times, he faked narcolepsy to stop me from greeting him— before opening one eye to check if I were still there waiting, amused by his antics. He did all of this in good fun.

One afternoon, while we were watching television in his room, I noticed photos of landscapes on his wall and asked about them.

"They're photos I took after I retired. I enjoyed traveling and photography, especially forests and rivers and hiking around scenic spots." In a moment of unusual openness, he said, "I didn't discover this until after I retired. I wish I'd spent more time realizing what I loved and pursuing it." He spoke about the achievements he had felt were so important and how he had pushed himself to accomplish something noteworthy that would garner the respect of his peers. Mr. Robinson had judged others by their achievements and judged himself even more harshly for the things he never actualized. Although he did his best to provide for his family, he did so in a way he thought was acceptable to others, but these expectations did not match what he wanted for himself. "I'm proud of my accomplishments," he said, "but I wish I'd made time to do the things I loved while I was still healthy and capable."

We spoke about spirituality, which often comes up with patients at the end of their lives.

"I'm an atheist," Mr. Robinson said. "I haven't given life beyond death much thought. I'm a scientist. There is no room for God in science."

We disagreed on our perspectives, which made for interesting debates and conversations.

As the weeks passed, Mr. Robinson lost weight and slept more. He could no longer play balloon volleyball, and even refused to watch, which increased his depression and melancholy thoughts. I spent our visits bedside, watching TV with him. Talking became more challenging as his oxygen needs increased.

Often, breaking the silence, Mr. Robinson said, "I don't know why my wife only stays a few minutes when she comes to visit. I wish she would stay longer. Well, I'm grouchy and irritable because of this chronic pain. Maybe that's why she doesn't want to be around me." He missed her, and his loneliness showed. He wanted to see his children more too, but they were busy with their jobs and their children. "They haven't got time for me," he said. "I understand that. Besides who would ever want to come to this depressing place?"

Each time he brought it up, I suggested that if he wanted his family to visit more and stay longer, he needed to speak up and say so—and let them know it was important to him.

He nodded but felt he could not find courage enough to be vulnerable and express that to them. "What would they think of me? They'd see me as weak mentally. Sure, I'm weak, but I want them to see me as strong. I don't want to burden them." Instead of being authentic and expressing himself, Mr. Robinson lived his life based on how he thought others would feel about him.

Although he rarely expressed it, Mr. Robinson told me one of his greatest sources of pride was his daughter, whom he and his wife had adopted. But she had made choices he would not have made, and her decisions went against the grain of social expectations. As a result, he was concerned about others' potential judgments of his parenting skills. He recognized he judged his daughter for the standards he felt obliged to live by. Looking back, he saw how unfair he had been to her. He insisted she was good and kind and he knew in his heart she would be okay.

I encouraged Mr. Robinson to open up a little with his family and share how he felt. I knew it would be hard for him. "If you can share this with me, you can tell them," I said.

He faked a nap and broke off our conversation.

One afternoon, I arrived for a visit to find his daughter there. She was crying, and Mr. Robinson had drifted off to sleep. She shared with me about the amazing talk they had just had, and how she felt whole. Mr. Robinson told her he loved her and was always going to love her. He told her how proud of her he was, that she was a wonderful mother to her children, and encouraged her to keep living the life she felt was right for her—not to worry about what others thought. When she told him she hoped to see him again, he replied there must be a God because He brought her to him, so that must mean they would see each other again. She told me it was the sweetest, most profound discussion she had ever had with her dad. She had written it down so she could always remember it. It gave her closure she had never expected, and she was grateful.

I suspected Mr. Robinson was not asleep, but why ruin the perfect moment of closure for them? He passed away a short time later.

Your world can be challenging. Expressing one's truth from the heart is fraught with challenges, for it forces one to set aside fear and judgment.
~ A-Team

Chapter 18

Welcome Parties

A s I noted earlier, most people give little thought to their death because it is too depressing, final, and scary to consider. At some point, however, someone close to us dies or we become aware of our own impending death. We feel under-prepared emotionally to process the event. But in my experience, a close encounter with our own mortality helps us see the world with fresh eyes. It shifts our self-centered perspective to a more grateful, present, and mindful view. We see the world in a more positive light and appreciate the small things.

As I also mentioned earlier, as death approaches, often fear holds the dying person back and keeps them from letting go. The body tenses, resisting rest as the person fears they will not wake up again. They want to keep their eyes open and hold on to every moment, even though they know their body is shutting down. As the end approaches, and the dying person finds themselves on an undeniable trajectory, they delay processing their impending death. Anxiety increases, as they stress about discomfort or pain, and their regrets at leaving all they love behind.

The truth, according to Spirit, is that dying is easy. The hard part is the fear and apprehension leading to one's transition. Dying is just a shift in focus away from our physical body towards a non-physical reality.

Suppose we allow ourselves time to consider our inevitable transition and to explore the wisdom and understanding that awaits us. Pondering our departure will ease some anxiety around saying our final physical goodbyes. We can then consider how we want to spend our remaining time and say and do things in ways that ring true for us (instead of fearing what others might think). Our perspectives can broaden with a greater focus on quality of time over quantity, and we can foster relationships that bring us joy and peace. We will find ourselves more altruistic and less materialistic, and we will recognize the blessings all around us. Then, as death approaches, our mindset of awareness and appreciation will open us up for a smoother transition and help us release our need for control.

This is an important time. As I have shared in earlier stories, death is often time for a party, and we are the life of that party. As beloved family and friends in the physical realm say goodbye, others in the Spirit world are waiting to say hello and to usher their loved one back again. As in Mr. Virgil's story, Spirit has often shown me glimpses of deceased loved ones preparing to welcome a transitioning Soul back to the other side. These jubilant scenes appear similar to how we envision a party here on Earth. There is a gathering of people (both with and without bodily form), and sometimes pets and other animals attend as well. Everyone is always smiling, and there is a feeling of anticipation, excitement, joy, and love surrounding them.

Usually, one personality is waiting to be the first to welcome their loved one, and that spirit person often has a special connection to the person who is dying. These leading personalities have decided— or were chosen—to greet and escort the dying person to meet the other beloved Souls waiting to shower the newcomer with love and excitement. Interestingly, as I observe these get-togethers, this lead person is receptive to my presence and lets me tag along. When I take part in these spirit-world situations, the feelings of pure bliss overwhelm me.

I am not sure if parties and gift-giving are a regular occurrence in the afterlife, but I know they are common during one's physical death. The people at this other-worldly event glow from within, emanating light. You cannot help but gravitate toward them with elation. Often, the spirit people come bearing gifts. The offerings range from hugs, flowers, balloons, and small ornate objects to something simple like a shell or a stone. Often, these items appear brighter or more intense than similar items on Earth.

The spaces where these celebrations happen vary. They take place in fields of bright, colorful flowers; in small cottages adorned in ivy; in lush, vibrant gardens; and even in all-white, bright rooms of light. The creativity for these party locations is endless and astonishing. For example, when I see a field of flowers, they appear larger and brighter than any field of flowers I have ever seen on earth. The gardens and vegetation glow with a life all their own. Even an all-white room appears brighter than anything on our planet. Sometimes these parties seem pre-arranged as surprise parties; others feel more like casual family reunions. It is unclear to me how those in spirit select these locations, but the guest of honor is always the transitioning Soul.

These gatherings often have a sound associated with them—typically a musical quality. Sometimes the music is a recognizable song. But most times, it is an indescribable, awe-inspiring harmonic musical tone. There is a calming, transcendent frequency that flows from these events. The space is filled with words, but I rarely see mouths moving. Often, the words that spirit people say are communicated telepathically, and they are imbued with feeling. I can pick up on these thoughts easily.

Sometimes I notice these parties weeks before my client's transition. When appropriate, I share my observations with those who are in the dying process and their families. One of my clients even asked me to relay to the gathering partygoers her requests for who she wanted to see there and what she wanted to do once she arrived. I found this amusing but followed through with the request. "You don't need me to convey your message," I told her. "Thinking about it or saying it out loud will suffice." This woman was a party planner in life and wanted everything to be up to her standards upon her arrival! After all, she was the guest of honor.

These gatherings offer closure and hope and release a bit of the fear that dying people can have around death and the unknown. It is a great honor for me to witness these parties and relay the images to the families left behind. Knowing about the celebration taking place on the other side brings them solace as they grieve for their loved one in this world.

Celebrate, for Love is all around you, even in spots you don't see, like thoughts, feelings, and intentions. It's a party of Love, a pool party! You float in a pool of Love. When you let Love in, how do you feel? Lighter? Yes, light enough to float. Remember to let Love in. Cheers.

~ A-Team

Chapter 19

Helen

One morning in late January, I had a vivid, precognitive dream. I was visiting my grandmother Helen and my Papa John at their home (although, in the dream, I never saw my grandmother and at this time Papa John had already passed to spirit). I had never seen this home before in real life. The house was on a small, gated and protected piece of lush, green property in the country. Animal "friends"—a goat, chipmunks, dogs, cats, birds, rabbits, a horse, a donkey, a llama, and more—filled the yard. All the animals got along. Looking up at the canopy of the trees, I saw that their leaves were hyper-colored, and seemed to glow. Each of the trees emanated light from within and were more vibrant than anything here on Earth. As the trees swayed in the breeze, they sang, making pleasing musical tones and sounds instead of words, like a beautiful background choir or a chorus humming.

Mom and I were helping my grandparents pack up and prepare to move. I asked, "Why would they ever want to move from this place?"

Mom responded, "Papa doesn't want to move. This place is heaven, but he has to help because Grandma wants to move."

Just then, Papa handed me a box and asked me to help. I asked, "Papa are y'all planning on moving out west again?"

He responded, "Nah, Nah. Here, take this," and handed me another box.

When I woke up, I knew my Grandma Helen would transition soon.

Grandma Helen was ninety-one and had endured the deaths of two of her four children, her beloved husband of seventy-one years, Papa John, and nine siblings. She had lost much of her joy.

Weeks later, my otherwise healthy Grandma Helen fell and broke her hip. After that, she declined rapidly. My cousin Candis opened her home to Grandma and anyone who visited to spend time with her. Gwen was with Candis at Grandma's side.

On June 2, I awoke to a Voice announcing, "Today's the day! Yes! You'll make it in time! Allow room for space and space for room." I was unclear what that meant, but soon I received a call from Gwen and Candis that our grandmother had entered the active dying phase.

When we received word about Grandma Helen's decline, Mom and I both hopped late afternoon flights from Texas to Las Vegas. Mom flew out of San Antonio, and I flew out of Austin. We were anxious to arrive before my grandmother transitioned. Our flights got delayed, but somehow, we landed at the Las Vegas airport within half an hour of each other. We rented a car and drove two hours south to Kingman, Arizona. Throughout the drive, Mom kept encouraging me to drive faster, but I kept hearing we would make it in time, so I did not risk it.

Earlier that day, other family members had come to say goodbye, but they had departed before we arrived in the evening. Candis, Gwen, Mom, and I stood around Grandma Helen's bed in Candis' guest room. She was unconscious, but her eyes were partly open. She had needed the TV on every hour of the day for the last thirty years, so we kept it on for her as she transitioned. The movie playing at the time was *Little Miss Sunshine*.

Candis and Gwen took a break around 10:00 p.m. Candis lay down and shut her eyes for a few minutes. Gwen went outside, and Mom found a quiet place to meditate. I sat at Grandma Helen's bedside praying.

As I centered myself, I felt a familiar weight of energy as those in Spirit draw near. Although I could not see him, I could feel Papa John. Then, the guest bedroom turned all white—clinical, but glowing brightly. I got the sense I was in a hallway outside a hospital delivery room. As I stood beside a door to my left, I knew my grandma was behind it. As I glanced around the hallway, I noticed another door at the far end of the hallway with a bright white light emanating from under it. Papa John sat outside the delivery room, waiting with me. Dressed in a 1960s or 1970s style—brown pleated pants, boots, and a collared shirt—he looked young and healthy. I did not know him then, but I knew it was him. He was beaming, overflowing with anticipation, and he exuded pure joy and excitement. I stood in this space, observing, and while I could not see what I looked like, I was aware of being in Candis' spare bedroom, with my hands on Grandma Helen's legs. Just as the Voice had announced that morning, I was leaving room for something else, Candis' spare room. I was leaving space to accommodate the change of our space into the delivery room.

It had been a long day, and I was tired. My vision faded, leaving Papa John waiting outside the delivery room door. I was aware of being in Candis' home again. I got distracted by *Little Miss Sunshine* and watched it for a moment. The scene showed the family piled into the van, and the grandfather, Edwin, was telling his grandson, in so many words, to live his life to the fullest now while he is young and not to wait until he is older… appropriate advice.

I thought I could rest an hour. Then I heard a Voice say, "We don't have that long." My vision of the spirit world quickly became clear, and I stood outside my grandma's delivery room again. I followed Papa John as he stood up and walked down the long white hallway toward another door glowing in the distance. When we reached it, he opened it, allowing even more light to flood out. This room was also all white. Behind the door were many people who had already died: Grandma Helen's sons, sisters, brothers, and many people I did not recognize. It was a celebration—a party with flowers and balloons. Everyone waited with anticipation. Papa John, with his hand still on the doorknob, said, "It's time." He chuckled, closed the door, and headed back down the hall towards Grandma Helen's delivery room door. Again, I followed. Then, I realized what his words meant: "*It's time*." I snapped to attention and was aware of my physical surroundings and looked at Grandma Helen. Sure enough, her condition had progressed.

I went to find Candis, Gwen, and Mom. "It's time," I said. We gathered around Grandma Helen, expressed our love and gratitude and gave her permission to leave. We reassured her we would all be fine, and she would be, too. Less than ten minutes later, she took her final breath. It felt peaceful, natural, and timely. She transitioned only ninety minutes after Mom and I had reached her bedside.

I am so grateful for this experience. I know Papa John and many others were waiting joyfully to welcome Grandma Helen home with love. The appropriateness of the delivery room and a welcome party down the hall brought me to tears. As we leave one existence, we are delivered into another. The boundaries of life and death blur.

Hello, old friend. Your desire to be where you are going keeps you from being where you are, little one. Fear not, you are secure, and life is eternal. There is no death. Choose joy, understanding, and release all fears and resentments, for you are always safe. Your life doesn't end because your physical body does. You continue as you always have, but you can move on with less holding you back. Forever (for that is exactly how long you have) is a long time to wait. Release what weighs you down.

~ A-Team

Part II

Science Club

Chapter 20

Introducing Science Club

One afternoon, I set out to understand time, the notion of non-linear experiences, and the concepts of past lives and eternal life. I walked into my bedroom closet, the quietest spot in the house for meditation, hoping for insight. I expected to have a conversation with A-Team, but instead, I was swept into an experience that was both transformative and exciting.

In my mind's eye, I saw a slender gentleman with dark hair and a small mustache. He was wearing a suit, and sat in a leather chair in a cozy study, sipping tea from a teacup. There were dark-stained wood bookshelves around him and a desk beside him. He and his study were in black and white. I have learned that when I see Spirit in black and white, it impresses upon me that the period I am seeing is from the 1920s through to the 1960s.

I picked up my pen and paper and, as I do when communing with the Spirit world, I recorded what I was seeing.

"Can you hear me?" the man asked. He had a British accent.

"Yes, I can hear you." I said, jotting down notes.

"Are you quite finished?"

"You're British?"

"Yes. Yes, I speak the Queen's English or, as I also knew it, the King's English." He seemed quiet, humble, mannerly, and a little awkward socially. I knew he loved hiking and chess. He uncrossed his legs, turned to face me, leaned forward, elbows on his knees, and said, "Are you aware of the Time-Space Continuum?"

I just stared.

"I thought not," he said.

I listened.

"It's imperative you learn this for future referral and reference. It will come in *handy*; don't you know?" He emphasized the word *handy*, like it was a double meaning or a pun, like the "hands of time." He said, "It's not bulletproof... there are *holes* in it, but it will establish a foundation for us to build on, and we can fill in the *holes* later." Again, there was an emphasis on the word *holes*, but I was not sure why. "That-a-girl," he said. "Something tells me this is the start of a great friendship. Jumpstart your readiness." This last comment seemed to come from him, but the words had a distinct cadence. There was a significant energetic shift, and the gentleman in front of me was different now. He was smoking a pipe, and I could not see his face through the dense smoke. It was as though he had become several people at once. This sounds unusual, but it made sense at that moment.

I was in my closet but knew I was also in another space, in the cozy study with these several united personalities.

Who are these people? I wondered. A third place of awareness flashed before me: I saw Elly May Clampett, a character from the TV show, *The Beverly Hillbillies*, on a farm. It made me think that one gentleman in front of me must have been great with animals and grew up on a farm. I heard "von Trapp ethnicity" and the word "hibiscus," and saw a hibiscus flower. This information came not from the man/men sitting in front of me but from somewhere off in another direction. It was as if someone had supplied the answer to my silent query to help me understand the collective group of men with whom I was communicating.

Then I saw a black hole, a spiral, and a lightning strike. These images flashed before me as I traveled through outer space, no longer in the cozy study. "Bohemian Rhapsody," a song by Queen,[2] played in my mind.

I heard an unfamiliar voice say, "Turbulence is hot air colliding with cold air." Then I saw two particles traveling fast in blackness collide and explode, emitting light. This let me know that one of the

---

[2] Freddie Mercury, "Bohemian Rhapsody," A Night at the Opera, EMI, Roy Thomas Baker, Producer, Queen, Producer (Rockfield Studio, et al., London, 1975). https://en.wikipedia.org/wiki/Bohemian_Rhapsody.

men before me must have contributed to a better understanding of turbulence and particle physics.

I heard, "Matter is harmonious like the piano in a concerto. It all must flow, and so it does." I heard "twenty-six" and saw the number 26 flash before my eyes. Then I heard, "All for now," and the men before me faded in a puff of pipe smoke. As I emerged from this experience, I felt as if I these people and places had been real (if not more real than what I perceive physically).

I am not a physicist or a scientist. My interests have always been more right-brained, so the experience left me with many questions. Wanting to know if the disparate visions and clairaudient messages I had heard meant anything significant, I decided to do some research. Following are a series of validations and explanations of every clue the Spirit world had given me—and boy was I in for a big surprise. Everything I had seen and heard made sense!

First, I researched British physicists. Could I find the man who had been sitting before me? It did not take long. I had never heard of him before, but his name is Paul Dirac. He was born in Bristol, England in 1902, during the reign of King Edward, followed by King George and Queen Elizabeth. He is responsible for an equation called "The Dirac Equation," which depicts the existence of antimatter and describes the behavior of fermions, a category of sub-atomic particles that are thought of as the building blocks of atoms. These can include (but are not limited to) electrons, leptons, and quarks. The Dirac Equation also depicts that what we perceive as empty space is brimming with particles. Dirac also predicted antimatter and contributed to the early development of quantum electrodynamics and quantum mechanics. He won a shared Nobel Prize in 1933 with another well-known physicist, Erwin Schrödinger, for new, productive forms of atomic theory.

Schrödinger's equation describes the behavior of quantum particles at any time or place in any position and the wavelike properties of matter. It helps predict the probability of events of a wave-function. It is also used to describe the interference diffraction patterns of the double-slit experiment.

Thomas Young was the first scientist to conduct the double-slit experiment, which shows that light and matter can have both wave and particle characteristics. A basic example of this experiment is when a laser beam is pointed at a plate with two slits cut into it. As the beam of light hits the plate, light passing through the slits displays on a screen behind the plate. The interference pattern of the light as it hits the screen show some photons acting as waves and some acting as particles. Through various double-slit experiments, physicists determined that photons and electrons cannot be both a particle and a wave at the same time and once observed, by a particle detector, they must choose a form.

Next, I looked up "Dirac" and "Holes." It turns out Paul Dirac proposed a theory called "Dirac's Hole Theory." This theory states that the continuum of negative-energy states, which are solutions to the Dirac Equation, is filled with electrons, and the vacancies in this continuum (holes) manifest as positrons with energy and momentum that are negative of those states. Even after researching this, I still do not understand what that all means. I am left with more questions than answers.

I searched the Time-Space Continuum online, and found Space-Time Continuum. It is a real thing, not a sci-fi movie term. A space-time continuum model has four dimensions: up/down, left/right, back/forth, and one dimension of time. It was Albert Einstein's work on special relativity that led to the combining of our Space and Time. In 1915, Einstein published his "Unified Field Theory of General Relativity" based on a four-dimensional space-time. Dirac's wave equation became a cornerstone of quantum theory in that it integrated Einstein's relativity into Schrödinger's wave equation, which describes the behavior of quantum particles at any time or place, or in any position.

When I heard "von Trapp ethnicity" during my transformative experience, I thought of the musical, *The Sound of Music.*[3] The von

---

[3] The Sound of Music, 1965, Produced and directed by Robert Wise, Cast: Julie Andrews and Christopher Plummer. Wikipedia. https://en.wikipedia.org/wiki/The_Sound_of_Music.

Trapp family depicted in the movie were Austrian. Still in research mode, I learned that in the latter part of Dirac's life, he taught at the University of Tallahassee and became close friends with a biologist named Kurt Hofer. Hofer was raised on a farm in Austria and was an extra in the movie, *The Sound of Music*. Hofer aligns with the image of Elly Mae Clampett, as he was a farm boy. The hibiscus flower turned out to be related to Mr. Hofer as well. His address was on Gulf Hibiscus Dr., and he was president of the Hibiscus Home Owners Association in his community.

Next, I researched Black Holes and Space-Time. A black hole is an area in space where nothing can escape, including light, because the gravity is so strong. A vast star can crush itself under intense gravity to such a small volume that it collapses into a black hole. Space-Time is a combination of three dimensions of space and one dimension of time. It was Einstein who theorized that an object in space with mass can manipulate space by bending it or pulling on it, and gravity is the effect of this. According to Einstein, that object's mass and gravity get left behind because of the extreme distortion of space and time around the object. As you get closer to a black hole, time slows down, and from an observation point far away from the black hole, time around the black hole appears to stop. This is called "the event horizon."

The spiral I saw could represent several things, but I feel strongly it could represent the Logarithmic Spiral as it relates to Space-Time. Also known as a growth spiral, equiangular spiral, and spira mirabilis, the logarithmic spiral's polar equation is $r = ae^{\wedge}b8$. Its radius grows exponentially with its angle. Another impression I had is that time somehow moves in a spiral, not linearly. The Lightning Strike and the Queen song *Bohemian Rhapsody*,[4] where the lyrics, mention weather phenomena like thunder and lightning and the astronomer, Galileo, made me think of this physicist. I researched Galileo to clarify. He is "The Father of Modern Physics."

---

[4] Freddy Mercury, Ibid.

Still interested to find out more about how my visions and clairaudient messages might relate to real science, I continued doing research. When I looked up turbulence and its cause, I found that the message I received that "Turbulence is hot air colliding with cold air" is correct. This more accurately depicts frontal turbulence, which occurs when a cool air mass meets a warm air mass, and a wave of wind is formed, pushing all objects upward. In 1926, Dirac laid the foundations for Quantum electrodynamics by discovering an equation describing the motion and spin of special relativity. Years later, another physicist, Richard Feynman, refined this theory, creating diagrams to simplify the math around particle interactions, giving the world tools with which to better understand the mystery of turbulence.

In my vision, I had seen two particles traveling fast in blackness, colliding, exploding, and emitting light. It turns out Feynman's diagrams depict a graphic axis that represents space and another for time. Straight lines represent fermion particles, such as electrons, and wavy ones show boson particles, such as photons. Upon collision, these particles either absorb or emit light.

The phrase, "Matter is harmonious like the piano in a concerto. It all must flow, and so it does," correlates to information I found about Paul Dirac. Dirac used harmonic oscillators, combining quantum mechanics with special relativity. Interestingly, he was called the "Mozart of Science," which relates to the piano concerto. Matter flowing is central to quantum mechanics because of Wave-Particle duality, demonstrated in the famous "Double-Slit Experiment." As noted earlier, in modern physics, this experiment shows that light and matter can be both waves and particles.

Finally, the number "26" is significant because Paul Dirac was twenty-six when he formulated the relativistic wave equation that led to the discovery of antimatter as anti-electron (or positron). Dirac combined quantum theory and special relativity to describe the behavior of electrons. This posed a problem in the science community initially because classical physics states that the energy of a particle must be positive. Dirac surmised that for every particle (positive energy) there is an antiparticle (negative energy) and that an entire universe made of antimatter exists. Dirac suggested a theoretical model, the Dirac Sea, to explain the negative energy quantum states for particles traveling near the speed of light. In this model, the antiparticle (positron) is depicted as a hole, which lead to Dirac's Hole Theory. Dirac's Sea Theory has now been replaced by Quantum Field Theory, but the math is still compatible.

Interestingly, Einstein was also twenty-six when he put forth his theory of Special Relativity. And it was in 1926 that Dirac laid the foundations for Quantum Electrodynamics with his discovery of an equation describing the motion and spin of Special Relativity.

My encounter with Paul Dirac and the events that transpired after he disappeared was unusual and exciting for me. It led me to research the information I received to see if I could validate it. As I confirmed many of the messages, it increased my trust in Spirit. Spirit gave me information that, while not new to the physics community, was entirely new to me. It was such an interesting group: Dirac, Schrödinger, Galileo, Einstein, Hofer, and Feynman. I called my new collective in Spirit, "Science Club." I asked Science Club to visit again if they had the time and space and told them I would do my best to understand their teachings.

Hidden inside you, in all of us, is the truth that we are all One, all Here, all experiencing, all Love.
~ *A-Team*

Chapter 21

Reincarnation

Reincarnation is a teaching in some religions (including Buddhism, Hinduism, Sikhism, and Jainism), and some philosophies. In these belief systems, when a person dies from the physical world, their eternal Soul reincarnates—it is reborn into a new, different, physical body. Reincarnation is often associated with karma, which can be defined as how one's actions may affect their fate.

Spiritual teachings express that we are born into a physical body, and as we grow, we make choices that affect us and others... and then we die and are reborn again. This continuous cycle of birth, life, death, and rebirth is called samsara. A Sanskrit word, *samsara* translates to English as *wandering* or *flowing around*. The life part of the cycle is where we experience suffering and karma. In order to end this cycle, one must detach from materialistic ways, discover self-awareness, and achieve enlightenment.

These teachings can feel limiting and unforgiving. What if reincarnation is more of a symbolic representation of eternal life? What if we are not forced to be in an endless cycle of samsara? What if we choose to experience a material reality for our own growth? A-Team has said often that we *get* to be here. We *choose* this. We can choose to accept our challenges as temporary experiences for our own learning, growing, and self-realization. We can choose to allow our Souls to enjoy and engage in all our experiences: happy, sad, angry, and loving. Accepting troubles and hardships and recognizing them as an opportunity to learn or grow—and even to be grateful for them—is hard. When we experience challenges, we focus on getting through them and solving or overcoming them. As A-Team once reminded me, where we focus is where we are. Learning to collect our thoughts and shift our focus around trials and tribulations can take a lifetime of practice. Some people find better flow through meditation, studying spirituality and philosophy, or trying out the healing modalities of western medicine, holistic wellness (e.g., hypnotherapy, sound therapy, past life regressions), and other creative practices.

Years before I explored hypnotherapy and past life regression (or as A-Team calls it, the other experiences of one's Soul), I had a couple of transformative experiences during meditation. In one, I sat eyes closed, when I spun out of my body into the cosmos. I was light surrounded by endless space but quickly became aware my surroundings were transforming into a room of golden light. Jesus stood there, waiting for me. His long brown hair fell below his shoulders, and a well-trimmed beard framed his olive-toned face. He wore warm, white robes of light and his brown eyes sparkled with flecks of golden light. I bowed my head in reverence. When I looked up and saw him bowing back, I bowed again. Without words, he told me he did not want to be placed on a pedestal—there was no need to bow. "We are equals," he said, "and no one is above or below anyone else." I felt humbled.

Jesus guided me to a giant globe. He zoomed in on New York City. As he did, I could see New York before there were any buildings. I saw it all "happening" in the 1800s and 1900s, in my current time, and even into the far future. I saw what appeared to be above-ground futuristic systems of travel, similar to railways, as opposed to the existing subway system. I did not see any cars or trucks. In the future, there were fewer streets than there are presently, and they seemed to be used almost exclusively for foot traffic. There were also underground travel systems similar to high-speed trains that could travel internationally, under the ocean. I saw parks, or what appeared to be green spaces, grown vertically on buildings. It was all happening in what appeared to be infinitesimal, thin layers. I could focus on a "layer" of time, touch it, and experience New York at that moment, but all of it was happening now in the same space. It was simply a shift in awareness. I could see all of it at once.

During another meditation, I connected to Spirit and was transported to a dark room. There was a round stone well in the center of the room, glowing with blue and white light. As I approached the well, I looked into the light, and I had a knowing that it would show me scenes from my current life and other experiences in other bodies as other personalities. It was a well of wisdom. I looked up and saw that there were other "Me's" surrounding the well. One "Me" was a middle-aged white man from Chicago dressed in mid-1800s attire. I could tell he was charming but that he struggled with compassion for himself and others. He was self-centered and focused on his career success. Another "Me" was a Black woman from the Northeastern United States experiencing life in the mid-late 1800s. I knew she had been enslaved, and she had challenges around worthiness and having empathy for others. There were two other "Me's" around the well, but they were blurry, and I could not focus on them. It was as if they were moving faster than my awareness could process. I felt they were experiencing lives in a time beyond my current existence. There were other "Me's" too—I could not tell who the real me was! They were all as much Me as I am. I even questioned if I were the real "Me."

As I will note later, time, while we perceive it as linear, does not really exist, so all the Me's gathered around the well were, conceivably, all existing at the same time—in the now. This strange and transformative experience helped me to understand the concept of being multidimensional and non-linearly connected. While I cannot wrap my mind around the concept of multi-dimensions, and the unification of distinct personalities into One, I at least have an inkling of what it feels like. Just as I experienced a knowing that every Me I saw was as real as I am, every fragment of the Self or personality that exists in the multidimensional world thinks it is the authentic Self. We are all real fragments of our Higher Selves, expressing simultaneously with multiple outcomes. Imagine a multi-lensed camera. The camera with its lenses are the Higher Self. The individual lenses are the various personalities or lives the Higher Self is experiencing. From various perspectives and angles, each life (or lens) contributes to the overall performance of the camera, or the awareness and growth of the Soul.

The Higher Self is eternal, and this current physical experience is just one of many experiences, or lives, we have lived and will live. As Spirit says, we are one life, having many experiences. The whole of who we are, our Higher Self, or Over-Soul, is a part of All That Is (or God). We chose to have an experience on Earth to express ourselves as a part of God, and in doing so, we allow part of our focus to manifest on Earth. But other parts of us focus in the realm or dimension we call Spirit. Our Higher Self focuses in the Spirit realm and guides the part of us that focuses here in our earthly realm. When we make choices, using our free will here in our physical experience, we impress upon our Higher Self the choices we have made that have influenced it energetically. In that other, spiritual dimension, our Higher Self recognizes our earthly lessons. Congruently, a choice not taken continues to unfold in another unchosen reality which adds to the understanding, awareness, and growth of our Higher Self. Most of the time this unchosen reality remains unknown to us because it is the path not taken. All choices strongly considered, taken or not, influence a timeline or reality and add to the overall experience of our Soul's growth.

After these experiences, I became interested in learning more about past life regressions and hypnotherapy, and completed certification in both modalities. However, after each day of training, A-Team would correct my hypnotherapy teacher. For example, the instructor was teaching us we were regressing, going back in time to an earlier experience and even farther back to access previous lives. A-Team asked me to consider another perspective. I am very visual so A-Team sent me an image. They showed me a tree. The trunk and canopy of the tree would be the "Higher Self" or "Over-Soul." The tree's roots represented the experiences of our Soul, or "past lives." One root, for example, was Gretchen, living in the twenty-first century in Texas. Another root was the Black woman in the northeast. Another root was the man in Chicago. A-Team said, "I am One life." There is only One life so I could not have *past* lives, because life is eternal. I could, however, choose to express myself and experience myself in different forms and circumstances all at once by allowing myself to be in many physical forms at once. Each of my experiences feed the tree's canopy through the trunk and contribute to the overall Higher Soul. Each one of my alternate expressions of Self happening in the now can have access to all our collective wisdom, because we are all connected. A-Team even showed our individual roots sprouting tiny feeder roots off our major roots. These represented paths and choices not taken, or alternate outcomes to the circumstances presented in any one expression of self.

These experiences have been life-altering for me. They shifted my perspective on life as I perceived it linearly and it expanded my understanding of past and future lives. I know we are eternal. We exist in more than one experience at a time (since time is not linear), and we are all connected and choosing our adventures. We are here together, learning and growing by expressing ourselves authentically. We shine bright in truth, and when we love ourselves, we cannot help but have love for others.

Be open to new experiences, thought processes, and beliefs. Remember that as you teach, you learn. As you learn, you grow, and as you grow, you feed your Soul's purpose and find greater peace and love within and for All. You are never alone. We are beside you every step of the way. Hold who you are up for the world to see and worry about, not what others think, say, or do. Do not doubt yourself, for your strengths emerge in self-love, self-expression, personal truth, and transparency.

~ A-Team

Chapter 22

Mr. Arjuna and Love Letters

M r. Arjuna was a fascinating man and one of my favorite patients. In my first interaction with him, he was in a wheelchair, friendly and chatty. But he spoke so quietly, he was next to impossible to hear. He was polite and concerned with being too personal or burdensome. I was Mr. Arjuna's hospice volunteer for four years.

For the first year of our friendship, he kept up the hope of one day becoming mobile, going home, and leaving the nursing home behind. He wheeled himself around in the halls and tried to stand on his own. I helped him stand and take a few steps. These were joyous accomplishments and cause for celebration. But it wore him out, and after a few steps, he needed to lie down.

We had many conversations about his childhood in India and his religious, Hindu upbringing. Mr. Arjuna questioned my beliefs, and we discussed theology and different religious philosophies. He was a spiritual man who closed his eyes, reflected in solitude, and engaged in regular meditations that some onlookers might have confused with naps. When he opened his eyes, he shared with me his wisdom and insights about our physical world.

Mr. Arjuna was very intuitive. Often, his words were filled with beautiful recognitions of the connection of all living beings. Sometimes he expressed regrets that so many people (himself included) did not always see the beauty in life's hardships. Mr. Arjuna said he did not believe in any specific religion, and over the years, that appeared to be true. But as his death grew closer, he settled firmly on Hinduism, the teachings of his youth.

Mr. Arjuna's beloved wife had passed away over thirty years earlier, and his Hindu faith had taught him he would not see her when he died because she would already have reincarnated. Believing this filled him with despair. He missed her and wanted to see her, but he also wanted her to be safely and happily reincarnated.

According to his doctor, Mr. Arjuna suffered from "hallucinations," and the doctors increased his medication to stop them. Some of these so-called hallucinations included what I knew were psychic visions and astral travel events, such as knowing his daughter's workplace had assigned her a new office (and describing it accurately) before she had informed him of this recent change. Mr. Arjuna insisted he had been at her office, even though he had never left the nursing home. Astral travel, sometimes referred to as astral projection or Soul travel, is a concept that our astral body (or subtle or light body) can project and travel without our physical body to other physical and non-physical realms. Astral travel is an out-of-body experience through which consciousness continues in an aware state without the earthly body.

I love this story because while Mr. Arjuna's knowing and his experience baffled his medical team (and his daughter), I knew his experience was possible based on my own intuitive encounters with consciousness. Other "hallucinations" included seeing his wife standing in his room, smiling and comforting him. Loved ones from spirit often visit their near-death companions to provide support. As Mr. Arjuna's health declined, visits from his deceased wife increased. He also had visits from other beings whom he did not know, but he enjoyed their company. He described them as helpful and kind and told me they hid themselves because they did not want others to see them. I loved it when he shared these moments because his visitors eased the monotony of his day and brought him true inner joy.

One day, I thought about taking my eight-year-old daughter, Elle, with me to visit Mr. Arjuna. I did not have a babysitter, it was time for our visit, and he was expecting me. He was not mobile enough to reach his phone, so I could not call to let him know I could not visit him that day. The hospice frowned upon me taking visitors with me, but I thought about settling Elle in the corner chair by the window with an iPad and headphones while I sat at Mr. Arjuna's bedside. I thought long and hard about it but decided against it because Elle would have had questions and the smells in the facility would have bothered her. So, I skipped my visit with Mr. Arjuna.

The following week, I showed up in Mr. Arjuna's room.

"What happened last week?" he demanded.

I assumed he meant I did not arrive for our visit.

"You brought your young daughter to visit me. You sat her down in the chair over there (he pointed to the chair in the corner by the window) and handed her headphones and a purple iPad." (How could he have known her iPad was purple?) "You sat down next to me. Then, without saying anything, you got up, walked out, and left your daughter sitting in the corner!"

Shocked, I said, "That didn't happen, but I'd thought about doing just that."

Deflated, he said, "Oh, I must have imagined it."

I explained I did not think it was imaginary. I do not think he understood the full gravity of what he had experienced and what I had planned. A-Team tried to help me understand this event:

Time and space are an illusion, a construct created to mark a beginning and an end to your experience in your physical world. They are a tool. Time and space help set parameters for which you get to seek wisdom and meaning in your existence. You are the creator of your masterpiece. In this physical experience, time, and space are the canvas. Mr. Arjuna's participation in transcending the confines of time and space was mutually beneficial. As the two of you co-create your own masterpieces, the wisdom and value for you both lie with a focal point beyond the material experience. Consider yourselves abstract artists, ignoring the boundaries and rules provided to experiment with a new perspective not followed traditionally.

On another occasion, I was sitting with Mr. Arjuna and had to leave. "Goodbye," I said, and walked to the door.

"Oh, you are back," he said.

I turned around and said, "No, Mr. Arjuna, I'm leaving now."

He said, "No, her." He pointed to my empty chair. "She sits with me after you leave so I won't be lonely," he said, flashing a sweet smile at the chair. I walked back to the chair, and to the invisible being bringing comfort to my friend, I said, "Thank you for keeping him company."

Mr. Arjuna smiled and appreciated my manners with his unseen companion. Often, he had visitors in his room whom I could not see, and I thanked them internally for being there for him. One afternoon, while visiting with my unique patient, he drifted off to sleep as I sat beside him. I used this moment of silence to pray and connect to All That Is. I expressed silently that I did not want to leave Mr. Arjuna because I did not want him to transition while I was gone. I still thought (wrongly) that it was essential to be present for loved ones as they took their last breath. Spirit suggested something beautiful and comforting that came in as a download of information. (A "download" is a modern word I use to help others understand what it feels like to receive an all-encompassing knowing about a lot of information in an instant.) They suggested I create a letter of love, "a Love Letter" for my patient. This Love Letter would come from my heart, thoughts, and intent. They also said that the love sent in this Love Letter would help lift my loved one to the other side.

I am a very visual person, so I envisioned an environment I thought Mr. Arjuna would enjoy: a beautiful landscape, with bright blue skies, a lush green field, and a waterfall. I infused the scene with my love, and with a thought, I captured that moment in time and space. I set the intention that when he transitioned, Mr. Arjuna would receive it and all the love it held in the manner in which I had sent it.

Spirit assured me there is no wrong way to send a Love Letter. I love this teaching and I create Love Letters for my patients, family members, friends, and strangers all the time. I make Love Letters for those I witness who appear to be suffering—people who have been in accidents, people experiencing homelessness, and those who are in grief. But, of course, you can create and send a Love Letter to happy, healthy people, too. I send them to animals and even plants and trees.

One late morning, the lamp on my nightstand was flickering on and off. This was unusual, so I acknowledged out loud to whatever energy might have been trying to get my attention that I was open to receiving their message. Minutes later, I received a phone call informing me that Mr. Arjuna had passed. The lamp light turning on and off was Mr. Arjuna saying goodbye… or hello. Mr. Arjuna had received my Love Letter. Joyously, I visualized Mr. Arjuna walking through the lush landscape I had created for him. In my vision, he reunited with his devoted wife near the waterfall.

Don't wait for others. You must push forward and walk the walk. In your world, action brings change. Step up. Push forward, for that's how you bring dreams to fruition. Time, she waits for no one, and this is a short lifetime on Earth that you choose, but one filled with great experiences. What you have agreed to collectively and have created is beautiful, and you get to be a part of it. You are a part of it. You can still create within your world by working within the parameters set and agreed upon. So, while experiencing Earth, you must make choices to bring about the change you want to see by playing by the rules. Although some rules can be broken (wink), there are always exceptions. You can see outward by focusing inward.

~ A-Team

Chapter 23

Here and Now

One day, when I was meditating, Spirit reminded me, "Know thyself." I am more than just a parent, a sibling, and a spouse. I am not restricted to this one linear experience. I am a Spirit living in more than one world and connecting with more than one body at once. As a Higher Soul, how boring would it be to be limited to one physical life? We limit ourselves when we believe this one life defines who we are (or who we think we are). After all, we have had many lives, or, as A-Team says, many experiences, each one taking place in a different moment in time and space. Each experience has structures associated with the social norms related to that time and place. In our current earthly life, for example, we deem certain behaviors as wrong, evil, or sinful. However, if we experience a life in a different expression in time and space, these same behaviors may not be considered negative. They may be an acceptable part of that culture or society. In Greek and Roman times, for example, it was customary for older men to mentor younger men and become their lovers. In our more recent history, the belief that homosexuality is immoral surfaced through religious doctrine and many gay people have felt shame and guilt around their preferences for years. However, our world is shifting once again and becoming more accepting, and fewer people cast judgment on the gay community.

Social norms and judgments vary greatly depending on the timeframe into which you are born. This is an example of our limiting beliefs about ourselves and others based on our collective societal beliefs. Our actions, good or bad, expressed in one single life do not define the vast and diverse Souls that we are. Every choice or moral judgment we make about the social constructs of our time limits us. We are multidimensional beings, after all, growing through our choices and experiences.

A-Team explained we make many choices in our daily lives that construct how our lives will unfold. Get married, or not? Move to a new city? Change our diet? Have children? Buy new shoes? Complete suicide? Every choice made means there was a different choice not made. But, as some quantum theorists suggest, that unchosen option is still expressing in an alternate reality that some refer to as a multiverse or multi-dimensional space. In this multiverse, all of our Selves are living and experiencing all the infinitive potentialities in our timeline. Spirit refers to these alternate expressions as realms or dimensions and has suggested that after we die, we will have access to records that show how our choices affected us and everyone around us, and how alternate paths not taken (but expressed in an alternate dimension) affected us and others as well. Regardless of the vocabulary used, the concept implies we are nonlinear (and so are our choices), which means that judging ourselves for the choices we have made is not in alignment with our multidimensionally expressive Selves.

Thankfully, this one life we are living is but a chapter in an unending book of who we are on a Higher Soul level. This Higher Soul is not a perfect, fixed thing. As it expresses itself through multiple aspects, our Soul is flowing, melding, and becoming. It is growing, expressing, and experiencing. We are more dynamic and connected to other aspects of ourselves, to each other, and to All That Is than we realize.

As I contemplated the teachings from A-Team that state we are not limited to our one physical experience, Dirac stepped in. He added, "We are only limited by the bounds of our own perceptions." He explained that by being open to the unknown, and by playing with new ideas and inspiration, we can build on concepts that may have once seemed far-fetched or inconceivable. Considering and allowing the flow of small ideas to build into bigger ones is crucial in recognizing our own potential.

Spirit says, "There is only here and now, and the power is in the *now*." This is a concept that many people need help to comprehend.

In our earthly, physical existence we progress through our lives linearly, in a cause-and-effect manner. Our choices affect the "progress" of our linear life. However, Spirit assures me that the choices we do not make are just as important as the choices we make. As noted earlier, our Higher Self, God-Self, Over-Soul, or Higher Mind (whatever term works for you) has access to all of our diverse multi-experiencing Selves. This means (since we are a part of our Higher Self) we can connect with all those same experiences. These (seemingly) divergent timelines connect like a web, branching out from one another. We can (and frequently do) experience inspirations and "bleed-throughs" or "run-overs" from our other selves, who are as much us as we are. As part of the Higher Self, each Self makes choices and alters their linear life's focus.

The power is in the now. We have the power to look back on a choice we made in our current life's past and change the potential outcome. While it will not change the past as we perceive it (because it has already happened and we have accepted it), in the greater reality, it is still happening. Since time is a construct, all the potential outcomes for every situation still exist in the present moment. So, we have power in the *now* to affect our future by shifting our perception of the past. We can think about the choice we want to change and replace that memory with a vision of what we would have liked to have happened. In doing so, we shift the linear dynamic. We can alter the choice an alternate Self made, and heal the Self in our current linear focus. The shift in perspective will alter our future timeline in a manner more in line with what might have occurred had we made an alternate choice in the earlier timeline.

You will need to do this many times, from a committed heart space. An example of shifting perceptions through time could be, "I would like to change my choice of not taking the job in New York." Now, you did not take the job, but everyone in your life, including you, has accepted that choice. However, you wish you had taken the job because of the financial security and inner strength that might have manifested if you had felt brave enough to work in a city far from home. Maybe you think accepting the job would have opened more doors or networking opportunities. Your focus becomes all the positive reasons you might have enjoyed the alternate experience. This centered thought aligns the present moment with what you want for yourself. Instead of holding on to the past as a regret, you rework it in your mind. Your mindset becomes positive, and your outlook attracts fresh energy into your field of awareness. New opportunities for financial security, inner strength, and networking will arrive.

We are always in the present moment. Our pasts are a series of memories of former present moments, and the future is an idea of goals and dreams we wish to manifest, but we are always manifesting and creating in the present moment. We never arrive at a future point in time because the future is just another present moment, here and now. Although we focus on our current stream of physical existence, other aspects of ourselves are experiencing their own narrow stream-of-consciousness. Time and space are irrelevant. Time helps us connect while we focus on our earthly lives, but its constraints, limitations, and boundaries do not apply the same way outside our single stream of focus. For that reason, we can connect to the past, present, and future and to alternate realities. It is all here and now. We are not limited to this singular physical existence. How many of us would be excited to find this is really all there is? No, we are so much more than this, and gratefully so. Time is merely a tool, marking the beginning and ending of a Soul's finite perspective in this physical stream of consciousness. If our perception of time did not exist, there would just be now. So, you see, time is an illusion. All there is… is Here and Now.

Our current physical expression is one of many lives we are living within a multidimensional multiverse. With this broader perspective in mind, sometimes a Soul transitioning out of its physical body is unaware they have switched focus from one stream of consciousness to another.

This can cause temporary confusion, but it is not a serious concern. A-Team explained to me once:

There can be confusion sometimes when a Soul crosses out of a body, a shift in focus, but not for long, and that Soul is never alone. None of us are. Sometimes a Soul needs a remembrance or a helping hand, but again, they are not alone. They are not stuck or lost. They may choose perspectives, as we all do, but they are always safe.

Free will and choice continue even when we do not focus on our bodies. Sometimes Souls will hang around, still interested in the life they just left. This does not imply they cannot move on. I liken it to sitting on the couch for a weekend and binge-watching a television series. We have placed our focus on the roles of the characters on-screen, away from the current events shaping the world. Life continues outside our living room, but we escape into the television series and invest in those characters for a little while. We are not stuck; we are choosing this experience. Likewise, some newly transitioned Souls enjoy observing their bodies, their loved ones, and the circumstances of others after they have transitioned. There are aware that more is happening around them, but they choose where to place their focus.

Sometimes, if there is confusion as a Soul shifts their stream of consciousness, they will try to make sense of their experience. It can seem illogical at first, a little like a dream, and sometimes they will ponder the circumstances of their death or pivotal, unresolved moments from their recent life. You can imagine it as having an altercation with someone, and then after the fact, you think about how it unfolded—what you should have said or done differently—agonizing over what you did or did not do. You do not have closure, so you recreate it in your mind, hoping to resolve it. In a similar fashion, seeking understanding and closure, a Soul will recreate an unresolved moment. It is a choice. But the Soul will soon discover that help with understanding and greater awareness is but a thought away. As Spirit has stated many times before, we are not alone. Sometimes we seek help from guides, teachers, psychologists, and mediums, and those no longer in physical bodies can choose to do the same. Each Soul has many opportunities to learn its lessons, in the spiritual world, in the physical world, and in countless dimensions of non-linear time and space. After all, time is more like a spiral, not a line. We are all sparks of God, experiencing and learning as we bring greater awareness to our Souls and contribute to the overall knowing and understanding of All That Is.

Time is. This is it. We are here. We just are. Just Be. (He draws a square box in the air with his fingers). Time is an illusion; it's not linear. It is set up so we can have a start and an end to experiences on Earth. Time isn't real.
~ A Conversation with a Council member in Spirit

Chapter 24

Reggie

One afternoon, I made a quick stop to visit a friend in the hospital. She was asleep, so I sat in a navy blue chair next to her bed and waited. A gentleman entered the room wearing a hospital gown and wheeling a mobile I.V. drip. He had a genuine smile and looked like he was in his sixties. I will call him Reggie.

"What are you doing in here?" he asked.

I assumed Reggie had entered the wrong room. As he walked toward me, the hospital room shifted into a glowing desert canyon landscape. Then it occurred to me he was not in his physical body. I had a sudden knowing that Reggie's body was a few doors down the hall resting, but his awareness had stepped out for a bit.

He exuded awe and wonderment. I felt an overwhelming sense of freedom, yet as he clung to his I.V. drip, I knew Reggie was not ready to let go of this physical existence just yet. Typically, when I notice a client outside their body, it comes with a knowing that they are ready to leave their body. Reggie was different. I looked around at the vast, orange and red canyon that sprawled before me. It was much larger than the room I sat in, of which I was still aware. Reggie sat down, swung his legs off the canyon cliff edge, and released his tight grip on his drip. He motioned me to join him.

I found myself swinging my legs off the canyon edge next to him, while also being aware of my physical self sitting in the chair. I was in both places at once.

Reggie gazed at the scenery before him in wonderment and said, "I am here."

I nodded.

"I am here, right now."

I nodded.

"I am also there." He pointed straight ahead, over the vast landscape, through the hospital wall toward his room. "I'm here with you, but I'm also there, lying in a hospital bed." He was in two worlds at once. "There is only here!" After a moment, Reggie stood up, so I stood up with him. "If I could be anywhere, could I be anything? I've always wanted to be a firefighter." His distinguished visage wavered, and his image flashed into a little boy, then regained its original appearance.

I was looking at the red canyon, reconciling in my mind, *that is also a hospital wall*, when I heard a ladder raising. I looked to my right, and Reggie was now in full firefighter regalia, scaling a ladder into a tree that I knew was not there moments ago. He looked back at me with a big smile, pleased with himself. He climbed the ladder higher and, stretching and reaching into the thick canopy, he retrieved a small gray tabby kitten. He climbed down the ladder, cradling the kitten and whispering soothing words to it. Once back on the ground, he set the kitten down, and it darted away. He stood there with his hands on his hips, still smiling, feeling good. He looked at me and declared, "We could climb the tree, and we don't have to worry about getting stuck because I can get us down."

I thought about it and the next thing I knew, I was up in the tree with him. Our view was amazing. The canyon stretched for miles, and observing it made me realize we are so small by comparison.

After a while of gazing out into the vast, beautiful landscape, Reggie the firefighter said out loud what I was thinking. "We are so small. Sometimes we forget how many other lives and perspectives are around us because we are so focused on ourselves. Rarely do we make time to leave our own points of view and observe, to just sit and observe in a moment without judgment or fear or without trying to save someone or fix something. What if, every so often, we could be like the canyon and just be in the moment supporting all the life around, without scrutiny? Just taking in the splendor and recognizing we are a part of it. Remember, we are part of a greater whole but are also made up of many other living parts, like cells and microorganisms such as bacteria, fungi, and viruses. All are alive, following their own life cycle, supporting our bodies without our conscious control. Such is the canyon, a grand supportive place home to millions of trees, animals, insects, and more. It is also a smaller part of a larger landscape and an even smaller part of an entire planet."

We sat a moment in silence, and then I heard the ladder again. Reggie the firefighter helped me down from the tree, and we stood on the cliff ledge once more.

"I've spent a lot of time trying to control outcomes," he lamented. "I got upset and anxious when things went wrong, but now I realize they didn't go wrong; they just didn't go my way. I've always been confident that my decision and choices were the optimum ways to proceed, but now I know that wasn't always the case. By needing to have my way, I had to show others their ways would not work. Convinced my way was the most efficient, I closed myself off to new ideas and perspectives. I always wanted to be the one with the great idea, the answers, the one people praised for being the hero. Rarely did I consider how being right made others feel wrong. I want a do-over, more time to get it right. I'm sure I could be a part of everything instead of trying to control everything."

It felt as if Reggie the firefighter was being guided through his moments of clarity, but I could not perceive who or what was inspiring his a-ha moments. I glanced at my still-sleeping friend in her hospital bed. My other reality vanished. I closed my eyes in prayer and tried to focus on the firefighter again. There was Reggie, back in his hospital gown, clutching his I.V. drip, heading back out the door. I glanced at the time on my phone, and while it had felt like a fifteen- or twenty-minute encounter, only a couple of minutes had passed.

A special place is this where we join together, for there is only Here. In the distance, you think you must go, but every step leads you to the same place. Here and Now. Every destination you arrive at is still always Here and Now.
~ A-Team

Chapter 25

Science Club Has More Members

Not long after my original meeting with Science Club, I felt an overwhelming need to sit and talk with them again. I found myself transported to another space just like before, only this time, I was in an old lecture hall theater with tiered seating in a university. The desks and chairs were wooden. Albert Einstein was standing at the blackboard teaching. Although respected and renowned, he came across as humorous. Einstein's peers filled the classroom. They felt like equals, and all of them listened, took notes, and contributed to class discussions. Everyone was respectful and respected. Some attendees were sitting, a few leaned on desktops, and a couple stood at the back of the room. Even though everyone wore suits, the atmosphere was informal. Laughter, serious discussions, and interesting questions were happening all around me, but I could not tune in to what anyone was saying. I thought, *Who are these people?*

I was aware of myself sitting at a desk, and alongside me was my new acquaintance, Paul Dirac, as well as several other physicists. The classroom was in color and I was in color, but the physicists were in black and white. Dirac looked at me and said, "Sometimes we all have to piggyback on the finds and discoveries of others. That is how we progress. Foundations are essential." I saw a pencil drawing of a squiggly line flash in my mind as if it were a note jotted down for me. "Waves are next for you to understand because they carry/transport energy/ information to be received. They are flexible and able to adapt."

Dirac impressed upon me we are all made up of light frequencies, implying that we, too, are carrying energy and information and can adapt. During this time, I saw triangles of various kinds forming distinct patterns, akin to a kaleidoscope. One image depicted two cones of light, one on top of the other, touching at their vertices, creating a form similar to an hourglass. A squiggly line ran through its center where the two points merged. Dirac impressed upon me that our bodies are comprised of many lights radiating outward as a cohesive unit. These smaller lights make up a pattern of energy, which can respond/react to its environment, and which flows with purpose, like a wave.

I looked to my right and saw a woman sitting next to me. Her hair was up and she was wearing a long skirt. She looked at me, smiled and nodded, making me feel like an expected, welcomed special guest. We were the only women in the classroom. I did not know who she was, but I heard the name "Marie." I am embarrassed to say it did not click for me right away. Later, I researched physicists named Marie and discovered she was Marie Curie, a well-known physicist and chemist who pioneered research in radioactivity. After years of research alongside her husband, Pierre Curie, Marie's colleagues recognized her for her contributions to chemistry and physics by awarding her a Nobel prize in both disciplines. She is the only person to achieve such an accomplishment and was the first woman to win a Nobel Prize.

Marie Curie discovered the elements radium and polonium. This was possible using a technique she invented that isolated radioactive isotopes. This led her to coin the term, "radioactivity." She developed mobile radiography units during WW1 to provide X-ray services in battle. Using her husband's invention, the piezoelectric quartz electrometer, an instrument for measuring an electric charge, Marie found that uranium rays electrified the air around a lab sample to conduct electricity. Because of this, she suggested that the radiation created was not the outcome of the interaction of molecules but that the atoms themselves created it. This was an essential step in disproving the idea that atoms were indivisible.

As I glanced around the classroom, wondering who each person was, I saw the cover of my dad's old Pink Floyd Album, "The Dark Side of the Moon," flash before me. The emphasis of the vision was on the glass pyramid with a single light ray refracted on it, producing a rainbow. The glass pyramid experiment was an early demonstration on light refraction and the color spectrum conducted by English mathematician Sir Isaac Newton.

Next, I saw an apple. This made me think again of Newton and the story about the apple tree and gravity, but Science Club impressed upon my thoughts that the apple was a poison apple instead. Someone handed the poison apple to a teacher. This was helpful so I would not confuse the ideas of the physicist they were trying to relay with the ideas of Newton. I researched "poison apple" AND "physics." A story popped up. According to a book called *Blackett: Physics, War, and Politics in the Twentieth Century*, Robert Oppenheimer, a theoretical physicist credited as the father of the atomic bomb, tried to poison his tutor at Cambridge with a poison apple. The administrators had placed him under the tutelage of Patrick Blackett, a physicist who later became famous for his work on cosmic rays. Oppenheimer, a graduate student, became jealous of Blackett. While on vacation with a couple of college friends, Oppenheimer confessed to poisoning an apple with lab chemicals and placing it on Blackett's desk. He told his friends that he needed to return to Cambridge to ensure Blackett did not eat the apple. Blackett had not eaten the apple, but the university wanted to press charges. Through Oppenheimer's parents' intervention, the university did not charge him and instead they placed him on academic probation.

Still in the classroom theater, I saw particles condensed together and then scatter and heard the word "plank." Later, I learned that Max Planck was a physicist from Germany who discovered quantum theory, which won him the Nobel Prize for Physics in 1918. His contributions shifted our understanding of atomic and sub-atomic processes. The first instance of an absolute law of nature that impressed Planck was the law of the conservation of energy, the first law of thermodynamics. Later, during his university years, he became convinced that the law of entropy, the second law of thermodynamics, was also an absolute law of nature. The second law became the subject of his doctoral dissertation at Munich, and it lay at the core of the research that led him to discover the quantum of action (now known as Planck's constant h) in 1900. In my vision, the condensed, scattering particles portrayed entropy.

I heard the words "triple ripple" and got the impression that there is a particle with wavelike properties that somehow also ripples. Researching this, I found information about a particle called the Higgs boson particle, sometimes referred to as the God particle. Theoretical physicist Peter Higgs and a team of scientists hypothesized this elementary particle. In the current description of our world, every particle is a wave in a field. In the situation with the Higgs boson, the field came first. The Higgs field fills the entire Universe and gives mass to all elementary particles. The Higgs boson is a wave in that field with a spin of zero. Because particles do not have mass on their own, they get their mass by interacting with the Higgs field. The stronger the interaction between a particle and the Higgs field, the heavier the particle ends up being. Elementary particles, including electrons, bosons, and others interact and acquire a variety of masses. Photons do not interact and therefore have no mass. Particles colliding create the Higgs boson, as CERN (the European Lab for Particle Physics) has shown. Physicists have also discovered a triboson, a triple boson. Perhaps this is the "triple ripple" in spacetime my vision interpreted.

I saw a blue light flash around me and heard what sounded like "chairecove." Later, as I continued my research on waves and radiation, I found a specific type of radiation called "Cherenkov radiation." It is electromagnetic radiation emitted when a charged particle (such as an electron) passes through a dielectric medium (an electrical insulator that an applied electric field can polarize) at a speed greater than the phase velocity (the speed of a wave in a medium) of light in that medium. An example is the blue glow of an underwater reactor. Scientists named this type of radiation for physicist Pavel Cherenkov, who shared the Nobel Prize for his discovery in 1958.

I also heard "fizz pop" (like a soda) and felt the words pertained to studies in light or radiation. I discovered there was a researcher by the name of Fritz Alfred Popp who studied biophysics and coined the term "biophotons." He discovered that all living organisms, including human cells, emit light radiation. An image of bubbles in space popping followed, and I had an impression it related to spacetime. This was more complex to research. After a while, I found articles discussing quantum foam. This foam-like field permeates the universe. Fluctuations play an important role in the ever-changing universe in which we live. For example, if we imagine looking at the universe from an eagle-eye perspective, when it comes to things bigger than an atom (like people and planets), Einstein's space-time is smooth. For our tiny quantum world, even seemingly empty space is filled with changes that resemble bubbles. Larger items cannot feel these tiny fluctuations, but tiny subatomic particles may experience them as huge. This theoretical quantum fluctuation of spacetime is called quantum foam. In quantum foam, particles appear and disappear spontaneously like foamy bubbles in soda. This effect was first recognized by Dutch physicist Hendrik Casimir. He placed two parallel metal plates near each other, reasoning that if quantum foam was real, then particles should fill the space around them. As particles can also be waves, there should be waves everywhere in our empty space. Since the plates were placed close together, only short waves could exist between the plates, and the longer waves would exist around them. Because of this imbalance, the larger waves would overpower the shorter ones and push the plates together. This experiment validated the existence of quantum foam.

There is another principle to consider in relation to quantum uncertainties—the Heisenberg Uncertainty Principle. Formulated by Werner Heisenberg, it states that we cannot know with certainty the position or speed of a particle with perfect accuracy because high energy appears to be lost in brief moments of time. The higher the energy, the faster it is lost. This is important because it suggests there are always quantum fluctuations in electric fields which impact electrons. These fluctuations are also present in the aforementioned quantum foam.

♡

As I sat in the "in-color" university classroom, another of my visions unfolded while the "black-and-white" Professor Einstein continued his lecture. I heard (in this order and as quickly as a finger snap with each name) "Tesla, Edison, Westinghouse, Stanley." Then I saw a picture of Benjamin Franklin up close, looking at a ball of light he was holding in his hands. A little girl was looking at the orb, too. Most of us are familiar with Benjamin Franklin, Thomas Edison, and Nikola Tesla, but I had to research Westinghouse and Stanley. What they all have in common is electricity: light.

We know Tesla for his contributions to the design of modern alternating currents. He studied engineering and physics and is responsible for over 100 patents. Because of his knowledge and ingenuity, George Westinghouse hired him as a consultant at Westinghouse Electric Company, which is an American nuclear power company that resulted from the division of the original Westinghouse Electric Corporation, founded in 1886. George Westinghouse needed a viable AC motor to complete his alternating current system. He was already marketing and negotiating a deal for Tesla's designs. Westinghouse pioneered the power generation industry in long-distance power transmission and high-voltage alternating current transmission. Thomas Edison invented electric power generation, sound recording, and mass communication and had rivalries with Tesla. William Stanley was an American physicist who held 129 patents covering electrical devices. A patent is intellectual property that dictates only the owner of the patent can use the invention legally. Stanley's patents ranged from incandescent electric lamps to induction coils, and he is notable for building the first practical alternating current transformer. He also worked for George Westinghouse as his chief engineer at the Pittsburgh Factory.

We know Benjamin Franklin for, among other things, his discoveries and theories regarding electricity. He even has the CGS unit of electric charge named after him. One Franklin (FR) equals one statcoulomb. The statcoulomb (statC) or franklin (Fr) or electrostatic unit of charge (esu) is the physical unit for electrical charge used in the centimeter-gram-second (cgs) electrostatic system of units. The SI system of units uses the coulomb I instead.

During this experience, I heard the term "platonic wave." I am aware of Platonic solids, but I could not find any research supporting platonic waves. I am including it here as part of the overall experience, and to maintain the integrity of the information coming through. Since the information flowing during this experience relates to waves, spacetime, light, and radiation, perhaps future findings will draw a link with this term and these related studies.

What an interesting classroom! So many scientists, all researchers from different points in our history, with various backgrounds who made many contributions to science—all of which have an underlying current for understanding waves and light.

When I asked Science Club why they met with me, an average person with little interest in or understanding of physics, they responded, "Because you asked for this." I suppose had Vincent van Gogh or Michelangelo stepped from the Spirit world to meet with me, I could have dismissed their teachings as information I may have read during college and retained. But having teachers step in from a field I do not understand strengthens my trust in Spirit and overrides the challenging question, "Am I making this up?" It helps me shift from expecting that only predictable things will happen, to embracing the idea that I can expect things unknown and astonishing to manifest in my awareness... leaving room for surprise, growth, and new ways of seeing my world.

Before ending our meeting, Science Club encouraged me to familiarize myself with a variety of waves—electromagnetic, atomic, light, sound, and radio—and to notice how, although they are all waves, they vary by speed, and when they increase and decrease, their energies become different. Marie Curie asked me to consider thought waves above all else, and stressed that thought waves are separate from brainwaves.

Upon researching thought waves, I found little information online that differentiates brainwaves from thought waves. Brainwaves are electromagnetic. The brainwaves are:

- Gamma – greater than 30 Hz – Focused, high-level processing
- Beta – 3 - 30 Hz – Active intelligence
- Alpha – 8 - 12 Hz – Bridge between conscious and subconscious
- Theta – 4 - 8 Hz – Daydreaming
- Delta – less than 4 Hz – deep sleep

That thought waves are not brainwaves raises the questions, "Are thought waves our own perceptions?" and "Does this mean we choose our perceptions based on the pattern of thought waves we have and choose to have both consciously and subconsciously based on our experiences?" This opens a Pandora's box of information that I could spend hours and hours researching, going down rabbit holes of information, theories, and ideas. I am grateful to Science Club and their teachings, and excited to be included in some of their meetings— to learn about science and its metaphysical implications in our spiritual growth and the importance of our thoughts and mindset. I look forward to continuing our club meetings and allowing the information to shape my greater understanding of the world around me.

Now that I have been introduced to the basic principles of physics, I am excited to apply these ideas to my metaphysical and spiritual practices and gain a greater understanding of my otherworldly visions and visitations in the context of the world of quantum physics. I am grateful to know there is a valid explanation for all I see and hear and I am curious to find out how this information will shape my experiences moving forward.

> Today is a day of great wonder. You sit with heightened awareness and in awe of such pursuits. It is thrilling, is it not? Your curiosity is piqued, but it has not peaked. Here, you have found answers, realizations, and questions; yes, today is surely a day of great minds and spirits... (My mind starts to drift, and I lose focus on A-Team's message). Wanderer! Your mind has shifted from wonder to wander. What will you think of next?
> ~ A-Team

Chapter 26

Thoughts

Energy *is*, period. Everything is energy. Thoughts are energy, too. Sometimes, those of us experiencing the human condition do not realize this. Thoughts are so powerful, they create things. Thoughts impact how we conceive our world, and our positive or negative emotions and desires create our physical environment. Thinking is a form of creation.

Can thoughts really have a significant impact on our physical Selves? I wondered. Spirit chimed in:

Yes. Thoughts exist abstractly. They are real. They "travel" in a field filled with information your scientists have yet to realize. Thoughts are not "just thoughts." They create worlds most don't perceive. They have impact and power. All creation does. You, of course, are part of that creation, and so are your thoughts. Loneliness, for example, is a feeling created by isolating thoughts. Joy is a feeling created from thoughts of connection and purpose. Indeed, thoughts are power centers for creation and shifts in perspectives. What if you thought of Love and compassion in your little part of the world? You could create that point of view for yourself and even those around you. Powerful indeed. What a gift. What a service. Some believe they have no impact on your world but are oblivious to their thoughts. Thoughts shift everything.

~ A-Team

♡ ♡

As Spirit mentions in the above quote, thoughts travel in a field of information scientists have yet to realize. *Could this be the quantum foam I researched earlier?* Science Club asked me to consider, *Where does a particle go when it disappears before reappearing?* I looked into this and found information on the collapse of a wave. Scientists say a particle exists in all possible states, but once a particle is measured or observed, observers can detect only one of its states. Once observed, particles choose a state—a particle of matter or a wave. I mentioned this briefly when I brought up Thomas Young and the double-slit experiment earlier. A particle disappears from observation in the instant it enters the slit and emerges in a wave pattern. Researchers have found that an observer effect occurs during this experiment. When scientists use an instrument or detector, the measurement of the experiment changes. Could this infer that all particles have a consciousness and respond based on who or what observes them? Do the thoughts of the observer play a role in the state of any given particle? Perhaps our thoughts affect even the basic, most fundamental properties of energy and the world we perceive. According to one theory, coined the "Copenhagen interpretation," a quantum particle exists in all of its possible states at the same time. Once observed, the subatomic particles collapse the wave function and emerge in a given state. This interpretation stems from the work of physicists Niels Bohr, Werner Heisenberg, and Max Born.

A person's thoughts and how they feel about themselves and their environment shape their perspective and affect the world around them. We all live in the same physical world, but each of us experiences this world based on how we feel about ourselves and others. Our perspectives can create anxiety and fear. Some of us are more present mindfully and can feel happy and content in any moment by expressing gratitude for simply being. Those who feel this way much of the time express positive thoughts and show us that happiness is a shift in perspective. But finding happiness can require us to create layers of positive thoughts, piling a series of positive thoughts one upon the next.

We are having a human experience, so sometimes our circumstances give rise to negative emotions, and we can let that negativity slip into our layers. Often, moments of negativity arise from a sense of separation from Self or Source. They can also stem from a sense of lack, usually about emotional needs that have not been met. But recognizing these negative thoughts and emotions is helpful. Understanding the beliefs that shape your negative viewpoints and feelings and noticing them is one way of transforming the layer into a positive.

It is essential to be aware of and process negative emotions. It is not about knowing you are unhappy and forcing yourself to fake happiness, hoping your depressing thoughts will dissipate. Instead, let all your emotions flow with awareness. Step back. *Why are you feeling these emotions? What are the reasons behind them?* Analyzing your emotions will help you adopt a healthier mental, emotional, and physical state. If you want to change your life, shift how you see and experience your personal reality and revamp your thoughts.

When we think a thought, the thought emerges as a wave carrying information that travels in a field all around us. This information can be positive or negative; about ourselves or others; fearful or loving. When you acknowledge your thoughts, take time to notice the positive in your environment: the good in yourself, others, and your world. This shift in perspective does not mean ignoring upsetting emotions—it just means honoring what is positive around you. Focusing on someone you love and are heart-connected to is an easy jumpstart to feeling happier and easing anxiety. Even the simple experience of enjoying the beauty of a sunset or the moon's serenity can shift your thoughts, moving you from a negative mindset to a positive one.

What you choose to focus on shapes your perspective of the world. Remember, your thoughts have power. Refocusing negative, fearful, or anxious thoughts and seeing the good around you helps restructure your worldview. First, acknowledge your thoughts. *How do they make you feel? How does it feel to notice your thoughts and feelings?* Seek to understand the fundamental ideas behind your negative thinking. *Does it stem from a sense of lack or fear? A perception of disconnection from Source? Can you turn that thinking around and remember where you have a connection? Can you be grateful for what you have?*

The contentment and happiness you engender by thinking positive thoughts or radiating gratitude also influence how you react in certain situations. Positive thoughts allow us to think clearly and calmly in stressful situations and help us process anxiety. You can tell a lot about someone's level of happiness and inner awareness based on how they live and express themselves.

In our human experiences, we want. We want Love, freedom, opportunities, a good job, financial success, a new car, a bigger home, children, and more. This is great. Wanting is how we co-create our environment. Because thoughts are things, wanting to achieve our dreams is essential. Not getting what we want or feel we deserve can create feelings of lack, compound our stress, produce prolonged anxiety, and create layers of harmful self-talk and negative perspectives. The trick? *Know what you want. Make efforts to achieve your goals, but first seek and find appreciation and Love at this moment, in the now.* A-Team told me:

> *Hello, old friend, you have a lot on your plate to process, do you not? Your desire to be where you are going keeps you from being where you are. Fear not. If it is to be, it will be. Look around and know you chose this, too.*

These words are a gentle reminder to find inner peace as you wait for your dreams to come to fruition. Being happy and content is not about achieving what you want. It is about being aware you are safe and provided for in each moment. It is about experiencing and expressing your contentment and seeking moments of awareness while you wait. We all have thoughts about what we want to gain or achieve, and we associate realizing these wants with happiness and joy. However, after receiving what we want, we move on to something else—we have a new want, we want to be happy again—and we rinse and repeat. Often, in our human condition, we seek happiness outside ourselves.

To practice realizing what my thoughts are and to reset my inner dialogue for positivity, I set the alarm on my phone to go off at different times on different days. When the alarm sounds, I stop and became mindful of my thoughts. Sometimes my thoughts are mundane. At other times, I am content and peaceful. But sometimes I hash out old arguments and experiences while in the present moment. During these times of thinking negative thoughts from past events, I imagine myself spinning on my hamster wheel of dissatisfaction. Then, to turn my negative thoughts into positive ones, I imagine myself stepping off my wheel and thinking of gratitude.

Spirit reminds us to reflect on our journeys:

Look at how far you've come. Consider where you are now. The Universe has always provided for you. It may be challenging, and you may not have all you ever wanted, but the Universe has always provided you with what you needed. You are still here. When you fall, we help you back up. When you listen with your heart, we guide you. Trust. Go all in. Choose love, freedom, creativity, exploration, and awareness over fear. Doors will open for you that you never even imagined. Dream bigger. You will conquer challenges as they arise, just as you always have.

Patience is a virtue. Can you wait for your dream patiently? Can you still seek and find joy in the in-between? Or do you miss it because you are so focused on what you want. Are you fearful of missing out on it to the exclusion of the now? Soak it all in. Don't leap before you can walk. Honor the choices you have made that have gotten you this far. Surrender. You have all the power to move past the heaviness/weight ... the wait.
~ Timmy from A-Team

Chapter 27

Mrs. Gabriela

One fall afternoon, NODA needed a volunteer to sit with a patient—Mrs. Gabriela. The volunteer who had sat with Mrs. Gabriella before me knew her family. He told me Mrs. Gabriella was a mother in her early forties dying of cirrhosis of the liver. When her children were young, she was a loving, doting mother. However, to cope with a series of unexpected life circumstances, she started drinking—and then disease took over. Through her illness, she felt angry and hurt and was a source of pain for others. She internalized guilt for her behavior which she numbed by drinking even more.

Her family grappled with their feelings too. They harbored resentment and anger toward her. It seemed the reason she was a NODA patient was not that she did not have a family; it was because they did not want to see her.

While Mrs. Gabriela's space was clinical, she had 80s pop music playing. The TV was on the Weather Channel on a rainy day, and the radar scope was playing on a loop. Mrs. Gabriela's vitals were inconsistent, and her breathing was loud and crackly. As her nurses monitored her, they chatted about weekend plans and friends. It was as if to them Mrs. Gabriela's death was a leisurely event.

I felt sad for my patient and knew I needed to center myself and recognize what I had come to do. Taking a few deep breaths, I set the intention to bring in Love, awareness, and peace for her. I turned inward, said a prayer, and tried to connect to something higher than myself. As I focused within, I saw Mrs. Gabriela standing outside her suffering body.

Mrs. Gabriela did not surround me with an incredible feeling of Love as many Souls do. She seemed happy to be free and out of pain.

Although she was aware of her body, she did not concern herself with it. I felt as if she knew I could see her, but it did not matter to her. She left the room through the wall and I stayed with her physical body. Somehow, while I could not see her, I knew she had not gone far. I could tell she was having fun, though. I sensed her wonder and curiosity.

About an hour later, six or seven people came into the room. Her in-laws, upset and experiencing conflicting emotions, wanted to say goodbye. I sat outside to give them privacy, but I was still aware of Mrs. Gabriela's Soul. She stood outside her material self, next to her extended family as they gushed their feelings toward her.

As I sat outside the open door, I saw Mrs. Gabriela's mother-in-law break down upon seeing her. I could feel her emotions as guilt, shame, despair, and anger overcame her. She hyperventilated, and an anxiety attack ensued. Her husband and son supported her through her emotions and grief. Although she felt guilty about taking attention away from her daughter-in-law, she could not stop the wave of anxiety washing over her. She tried to say she was fine, but eventually she expressed her feelings of anger and guilt for all to hear. She surrendered to the experience and breathed through her anxiety. After her episode passed, she re-focused her attention on Mrs. Gabriela.

By watching their interactions and listening to their confessions to one another, I realized that Mrs. Gabriela's family was not avoiding her because they were unsympathetic and unwilling to forgive her— they were heartbroken. They struggled to move past their thoughts of blame and pain. They loved her, had a hard time accepting her disease, and felt that her life being cut short was needless for her, her children, and their family. They had, however, found the courage to come in and say goodbye. They wanted to offer forgiveness, both to her and to themselves. They were unsure whether Mrs. Gabriela could hear them, but I knew she received the information and felt their Love because I could see her standing among them.

Sometime later, before they got on the elevator, I saw Mrs. Gabriela's mother-in-law take a deep breath, exhale, and dry her tears. Through my clairsentience, I felt her thoughts became more peaceful. She had needed the opportunity to say goodbye, to surrender to her grief, and perhaps on a Soul level, she knew Mrs. Gabriela received the message.

This story reiterates that the Soul is not suffering at death. The body is shutting down, but the Soul is revving up. It reminds us how important it is to love all our aspects—the dark and the light, the happy and the sad. It also reminds us we should not judge or try to change others. We can only change ourselves. If someone feels inspired to change and requests help, we can help them, but if they are not ready to change, who are we to say they need to? Instead, we can honor their journey for the growth experiences it offers them.

This story also shows the resilience of people. When they have the courage to be fearless and say what they need to say, even through episodes of panic and anxiety, expressing themselves openly and vulnerably, peace follows. Shifting our angry, hurt thoughts to forgiveness and peace is beneficial to all.

As bereaved family members reflect on their loved one's death, remembering they expressed themselves is comforting. It is a form of closure. We seek answers to help us resolve and come to terms with the loss of someone dear. The important, meaningful relationships that bring us fulfillment can leave us empty when they are gone. Closure, offered before or at the time of death, is a form of acceptance that allows us to walk through the grieving process with greater inner peace.

You can't change someone, and why would you want to? Who are you to say someone needs to change? We are all equally beautiful in the eyes of God, of All That Is. Believe it. Your way of living is not somehow better than someone else's. It's all experiences. Know that all is in order, and you can own your choices, recognize your actions, and learn from them. Life is not meant to be perfect. It is like a mirror, reflecting to us what we want to change and what we want to keep. Challenges are the fun part, we promise.
~ A-Team

Chapter 28

Children and Spirit

What does it mean to be a spiritual person? It means you are in a transcendent relationship with something greater than yourself, such as God, the Universe, or even Nature—something that is awe-inspiring and leaves you filled with wonder and gratitude. Many of us carry this sense of the divine with us throughout our lives. As children, we possess this awareness. Children are spiritual beings and often appear more sensitive to perceiving the Spirit realm than many adults. That is because unless we work on maintaining the relationship with the divine, adulthood's demands move our focus to our immediate physical reality and away from our natural connection with the spiritual world.

Children have a rich inner world that is not driven by responsibilities to the outer world. They are not concerned with endless mind chatter about bills, bosses, money, appearances, expectations, body image, or providing housing or meals for others. They are not subject to many of the daily stressors of most adults. Instead, they contemplate the caterpillar, marvel at the stars, conquer climbing a tree, and watch the world go by. The openness and ease with which children interpret the world around them is spiritual by nature. But why are children attuned in this spiritual way?

Scientists have tried to understand spirituality by measuring brainwaves. As I mentioned earlier, brainwaves are electrical impulses in the brain that allow for communication between billions of neurons. To recap, the frequencies in which brainwaves exist are:

- Gamma: greater than 30 Hz. It is a state of focused high-level processing, and problem solving.

- Beta: 13-30 Hz, which is our operational intelligence mode; it allows us to learn new tasks and have active conversations.
- Alpha: around 8-12 Hz. It is the bridge of conscious and subconscious. In this state we are relaxed and creative.
- Theta: a frequency of only 4-8 Hz. We enter this state when we are daydreaming or in deep meditation.
- Delta: less than 4 Hz. This where we find deep sleep.

As children, we operate at lower frequency brain waves for more extended periods of time, and the older we get, the more often our brains work in the higher brain wave states. Research shows that babies operate in the Delta frequency until age two, which is why they slip in and out of sleep. Between two and six, children progress primarily to the Theta state and can remain there up to age thirteen. This frequency is imperative for imagination and dreaming. It is also where a connection to Spirit becomes accessible. Without the frequent brainwave patterns of Beta or Alpha, young children cannot analyze or judge their thought processes—the information that arises in their minds is present and available. Therefore, they can receive extra-sensory information and wisdom readily, and can even see Spirit. This otherworldly perception is not yet outside their rational mind's interpretation. If children experience these spiritual moments and share this information with the adults around them, and an adult tells them they are imagining it, their brain forms a pathway that blocks what they know to be accurate. If an adult supports their perception, the pathway broadens and gets stronger. So, parental input shapes how children approach the world and how much information they interpret intuitively.

Children past eight years old spend more time in the higher brainwave states and start using critical thinking skills. This new frequency often overrides their imagination and the intuitive nudges they receive from Spirit or their Higher Self. And despite their parents' supportive or obstructive attitudes, by age ten, children have learned how and what to share within their communal group—and their peer group influences their behaviors.

In our Western society, instead of recognizing and honoring Spirit and its intuitive guidance, we often teach children that such experiences are imaginary. What if we considered that the experiences of our children, imaginary or not, were an opportunity to allow kids to process the world around them as it filters through their minds? It is more common, in our part of the world, to dismiss children's intuition and insist on them perceiving only what we deem to be "reality." What if instead we open our adult selves up to the possibility that more exists beyond our physical five senses? What if we ready ourselves to learn from our children?

Of course, I am not confusing imaginary play with spiritual experiences. For example, in my daughter's preschool class, the students imagined that chickens with magenta-colored feathers will lay magenta-colored eggs. What fun! Most children understand there are no magenta chickens or eggs, but it is great to be creative and pretend. So, I am not referring to children letting their imaginations run away with them, I am referring to the wisdom, worldly interpretations, and inspiration that children can glean from having spiritual experiences.

For example, while one of my clients was dying, her young grandson announced gleefully that Raz, his grandmother's deceased German shepherd, was playing with a squishy ball next to the bed and was waiting to play with Grammy. The family was not talking about Raz or even about other deceased loved ones. His comment appeared to come from out of the blue. No one else could see Raz, but her grandson laughed at the sight. The boy's father tried to convince him that Raz was in heaven and not by Grammy's bed. The boy looked confused but said nothing more. His grandmother passed shortly after that, and the family left the hospital. Of course, there is no scientific proof that Raz was beside the bed, but we limit ourselves when we shut down the idea that he could have been, just because we cannot perceive him with our own eyes. We cannot see the wind, ultraviolet light, or Love either, yet all of them exist.

So, is there a way to prove that these extrasensory experiences of spiritual phenomena exist? Science and religion appear to be worlds apart, but by using psychedelics, meditations, and visualizations, scientists have been able to induce spiritual experiences in study participants. Through studies, researchers have found that a spiritual experience activates the pleasure centers in the brain, and the results are long lasting on the mental and emotional health of the experiencer. During these experiments, the scientists used MRI (magnetic resonance imaging) and EEG (electroencephalogram), to measure brainwave frequencies and study the areas of the brain that light up during these practices. When one area, the prefrontal cortex (located at the forehead) is active, it reduces anxiety and gives a feeling of overall well-being. At the very least, having a spiritual practice appears to be a positive influence on our state of mind, our openness to the world, and our health. Developing this area of the brain also stimulates our creativity, reasoning skills, perseverance, and impulse control. We increase our overall feeling of balance and wholeness and build a stronger foundation of our sense of Self.

There is much about spirituality science has yet to validate or disprove beyond a reasonable doubt, including God, angels, spirits, and more. However, the scientific pursuit of knowledge and the fun and joy of conducting creative experiments to better understand ourselves and our planet *is spiritual*. It induces wonder, inspiration, and creativity. While it is easy to stay secure in a bubble of limiting beliefs, pushing the bounds of our ideas and concepts and going deeper into the unknown to gain greater understanding is courageous and exciting. That is one thing scientists, explorers, and spiritual people have in common: they all seek the truth and creative ways to explore.

When you wade in shallow water, you feel safe. But do you dare to go deeper? It is darker and colder, but much more life awaits you there. Be brave, be bold, and know you are always safe.
~ A Team

Chapter 29

Grandbob

My Grandbob passed away long before I started serving the dying community. His death was not a surprise, but it left our family heartbroken. My dad loved and respected his father.

Grandbob was a tall, dignified man who liked things a certain way. Although he could be uncompromising and stubborn, he also loved exploring, and took trips all over the country with Grandmom. He had a sweet tooth, loved audiobooks, and had an appreciation for nature, animals, fishing, and diving. He was also a woodworker who crafted beautiful chests and boxes as gifts for his children and grandchildren. For most of his life, Grandbob ran a family business and was an active member of his community.

Doctors diagnosed Grandbob with dementia and macular degeneration. Both diseases contributed to many moments of frustration and difficulty surrounding his care, which Grandmom provided. Near the end of his life, Grandbob rarely spoke, could not see, and was confined to a wheelchair. This was a significant shift from his strong, upright stature.

In the weeks before his transition, many family members visited Grandbob to say goodbye. He was one of the first great losses in our immediate family, so we honored his death with lots of love and goodbyes. As the end grew close and Grandbob entered the actively dying stage, loved ones surrounded him. I was not there. I was at home with my then-four-year-old son, Ty.

Taylor traveled for work internationally, and I ran the family business while he was away, all the while trying to balance out my responsibilities as a young mother. My situation was not unlike many others', and finding work-life balance is something to which all parents can relate. Every time Taylor traveled, I was extra vigilant, double-checking the locks on the doors before bedtime and triple-checking that I had set the alarm. Being home alone with Ty made me feel vulnerable and increased my alertness. I heard every noise in the house: the clink of the icemaker, the rumble of the air conditioning unit turning on or off, or the thump of our cat, Maxx, leaping from one surface in the house to another. For peace of mind, I let Ty sleep in my room with me, which helped me not to overthink every little sound.

One night in January, I had just finished my evening routine of checking and double-checking the house, when I received a phone call from my dad. Grandbob would not make it through the night. I told both Dad and Grandbob I loved them, hung up the phone, and got Ty ready for bed. He watched TV while I prayed for Grandbob. It was late, around midnight, before we turned off the TV.

As I leaned over to turn off the lamp on the nightstand, Ty said, "Mommy! There's a man in our room."

My heart pounded. My eyes darted around the room. I did not see anyone. *Have I locked someone dangerous in the house with us?* I tried not to sound fearful. "Where?"

Ty pointed. "Over there, by the window."

There was no one there. I exhaled and relaxed because I knew Ty was seeing Spirit, not an intruder. "What does the man look like?" I asked.

"He's got silver hair, he's wearing a suit, and he's standing tall and straight."

I eased onto the pillows on my bed. The man's description matched Grandbob's physical appearance. I guessed he was stopping by to say goodbye. Ty had only known his great-Grandbob hunched over in a wheelchair, so he may not have realized he was seeing the healthier, stronger version of Grandbob.

Ty scooted up next to me, took my hand in his, laid it on my heart, and said, "Don't worry, Mommy, everything is going to be alright."

Thankful, I noted how sweet and unusual his little gesture was. I rolled over and turned off the light, uneasy over the evening's events.

The following morning, Dad called and told me that Grandbob had passed away last night around midnight. "That's interesting," I said. "Ty reported seeing a silver-haired man in the bedroom wearing a suit, but I couldn't see him."

"What do you mean?" Dad asked.

I relayed the story as it had unfolded. Dad was quiet on the phone. I thought maybe the phone call had dropped. Instead, he cleared his throat. He was a little choked up.

"Last night," he said, "As I sat with Grandbob saying goodbye, I took his hand in mine, laid it on his heart, and said, 'Don't worry, Daddy, everything is going to be alright.'"

We were in awe of the beautiful synchronicities that transpired through the actions of a four-year-old boy to his mother, and a grown son to his father. The wonder surrounding this experience stayed with us and brought us peace. Dad could never explain it. After that, he could not say that "nothing happens after we die." It gave him hope that perhaps something more exists; that this physical life is not all there is.

Grandbob did an excellent service to so many of us by offering that experience through Ty.

Children are innocent, open, unlimited sources of creativity and love. Their wisdom is often overlooked, but they are Souls, just as we are and always have been. They may learn from us, the adults, how to manipulate matter in physical space by tying shoes, chopping an onion, or changing a tire. However, they can still relay deep wisdom and stimulate our imaginations through observations. They are our teachers, too.

Dearest little one, relax. You are in safe hands. You always are. There is no other way. Your wants and desires outweigh, at times, your ability to sit still and allow information and connection to flow. Play, pretend, and make-believe that all time and your ability to receive transmissions ceased. What would you do? You would stop and mindfully feel the world you inhabit, the world you create. You would seek a connection to something, to someone. It's who you are, who we all are. You are like a child in preschool, lollygagging and falling out of line, in need of a little guidance and hand-holding at times, but what a joy you are to behold. You are curious, and we love your sense of wonder, even if it causes you to wander.

~ *A-Team*

Chapter 30

Science Club Meeting on Sound

A few months after our initial meeting, Science Club held another impromptu forum. During an informative meditation with A-Team, while we were discussing ways to promote peace for a client using sound bowls, Paul Dirac and Kurt Hofer interrupted. Songs from the soundtrack, "The Sound of Music"[5] entered my awareness. I heard, "Sound is in everything." I responded with, "Except for space."

"You're wrong," they told me.

Their statement confused me. Sound is vibrations that travel through a medium such as air or water. Frequency is a sound measurement. 1 Hz = 1 vibration per second. Since sound requires a medium in which to be heard and there is no air or water in the vacuum of space, to me, it stood to reason there is no sound in space. Researching this later, I found that teams of scientists are using high-tech tools and telescopes to interpret sounds in space around black holes and other celestial bodies. Once again, Science Club surprised me.

Hofer chimed in with, "Everything is vibrating, including every cell in our bodies. Every living thing is comprised of cells, and these cells have their own sound of music that they oscillate at." He suggested sound waves could affect the pattern and behavior of the functions of cells. He told me we are only beginning to understand the depth sound plays in our physical reality. Acquiring a greater understanding of sound as a healing tool is life-altering, and there is beauty and resourcefulness in using sound to shape and improve our physical reality.

---

[5] The Sound of Music, Ibid.

Sound is the key to the universe and unlocks levels of awareness that have yet to be discovered. It moves through, shifting and changing, and influencing matter as we perceive it. It affects everything, even on a molecular level. Hofer explained that there is still much work to be done in the realm of sound, and that it is an exciting, blossoming technology that still holds many discoveries. We are only beginning to understand the depth sound plays in our physical reality.

Kurt Hofer was a biologist in his physical life, so I found it interesting that he was using his knowledge of cells (and his role as an extra in "The Sound of Music") to impress upon me the importance sound plays on a cellular level.

Dirac interjected, saying that "matter is harmonious." According to our current understanding, an atom, the basic building block of matter, comprises neutrons, electrons, protons, and 99.99 percent of an atom is waves of energy generating an electromagnetic field. This means it is vibrating at a certain frequency and pattern we distinguish as matter. Matter is not something physical; it is a certain level of vibration we perceive. Although atoms and the surrounding space can seem empty, they are filled with unseen wave functions and invisible fields waiting to be observed and interpreted.

Our universe is made up of waves, particles, and fields that vibrate, becoming distinguishable through observation and intent. Since all matter comprises particles and waves, information being transferred through vibrations fills the surrounding space. Dirac said that sound is mathematical; it is geometric. He explained that both light and sound waves, along with invisible fields, dictate how we live in our world and how we perceive others in it.

Wow, I said to myself. *So, it is essential to be mindful of our words because our voice is the sound that interacts with the vibration of our own electromagnetic fields. Our mouths and minds create waves through our words and thoughts. These waves vibrate at different frequencies, and the surrounding universe responds to them. Our body and brain are tuning in and resonating with the vibrations of the world.We both send and receive these waves of information and shape our lives accordingly.*

I was still feeling the presence of Dirac and Hofer when a new personality emerged. I heard Beethoven's "Symphony No. 5" with a man's voice singing the starting notes, "Bohm Bohm Bohm Bohmmmm." I saw the flash of an American flag waving in the background as a clean-shaven man with dark hair and tanned skin, wearing a suit, stood before me. His ears and nose were prominent facial features. He chuckled and said he was ready to be observed and that our brains are mathematical machines interpreting information, which travels on waves, and affects us on a cellular level. He said our brains both create and interpret signals which allow waves to come into coherence or synchronize with others around us. This ability to blend with others opens a greater sense of understanding and awareness, not only of ourselves, but of our relation to others. *Can choosing positive conversations or actions toward others stimulate brainwaves that can have helpful, healing effects on a cellular level?* I wondered. Later, I googled "physicist named Bome," and the first article I found suggested David Bohm. I researched further and learned David Bohm was an American-born physicist who worked alongside Oppenheimer, Einstein, and Weinberg (to name a few). He contributed to the fields of quantum mechanics and relativity.

Science Club is helping me to understand how our inner and outer worlds connect and affect everything else, from the microscopic to the macroscopic. Besides this, as I sit to interpret their messages, they are learning and experiencing, too. When I asked A-Team how Science Club is benefiting from our meetings, A-Team said they are working and experimenting on levels I cannot comprehend in my current state. A-Team also said we are all learning together how to blend or come into coherence with each other energetically to send and receive information. Science Club is continuing with work they started in their physical lives but did not finish and they are assisting our physical world for the benefit of humanity. A-Team says Science

Club communicates on a variety of levels with many people and our meetings are but a tiny part of their work. We are helping each other. It is part of our purpose in our life's experience not only to serve ourselves but to serve others as well. The better we understand ourselves, one another, and the way the world works, the better we will be able to serve others.

One way to understand ourselves better is to allow ourselves access to music and sounds. Hearing music increases the blood flow to our brains and lights up our limbic systems. Music can elicit different emotions and feelings within us. Therefore, music is something we feel. Having a greater understanding of emotion allows us to connect to others by communicating our feelings coherently, avoiding or resolving conflicts, and moving past hard feelings easily. When we expose ourselves to rhythms or beats in music or drums, our brains try to match the beat. Studies show that when people gather and listen to the same sounds or music, their brainwaves synchronize. During this process, there is coordination in body movements and the thinking processes of those gathered in the group. So, music is also controlling our brains' sensory perception. This helps neurologists like R. Douglas Fields understand how drums bring tribes together in ceremony, why song infuses religious worship, and why speech is also rhythmic.[6] When we hum, meditate, chant, and sing, we heighten our thoughts and affect our consciousness levels and those of people around us. Sound can affect our nervous systems, slow our heart rates and breathing, shift our brainwave states, and help us align with a focused flow state, which settles feelings of frustration and anger.

Often, professionals use music or sound to guide people into altered states of consciousness. Shamans use a drum. Tibetan monks use chants. Aboriginal tribal leaders in Australia use the didgeridoo.

---

[6] R. Douglas Fields, "The Power of Music: Mind Control by Rhythmic Sound," Scientific American (19 Jan. 2012), https://blogs.scientificamerican. com/guest-blog/the-power-of-music-mind-control-by-rhythmic-sound/#:~:text=The%20EEG%20recordings%20showed%20that,beat%20 in%20the%20drum%20rhythm. Accessed 11 Nov. 2023.

The rhythms and beats these cultural ceremonies generate create a common frequency which resonates with those listening. They shift a group into a calmer state of consciousness, aligning the group to the Theta brainwave state. Coming into resonance with others reminds us we are all connected, all one. We also recognize that serving others helps us, too.

When there is no foundation on which to build, there can be no understanding. These ideas and concepts can remain only theories. Proving a theory is another thing altogether. Physicists theorize, experiment, work, and rework until they find the truth as close as they can get in the data. Then, change can happen. It's already been the way it is/was all along, but an experiment can help one realize it/understand it. It changes nothing except minds. It is the way it always was. Sometimes we forget the importance of theories. They aren't proven, so they are more easily dismissed, but this is where the magic is. With the right/aligned heart and right/aligned head, one can solve puzzles, bringing about shifts in thinking and advancements in technologies that move humanity forward. We are not in control. However, we can still choose our outcomes. There is still so much left untapped, so much to be discovered. Great minds both seen and unseen are making giant leaps forward and advancements.
~ A-Team

Chapter 31

Sound and Music

Sound. Many of us take it for granted. As noted earlier, sound is a mechanical, radiant energy transmitted by waves creating vibrations that travel through the air or another medium. Sounds shape our perceptions and influence our environments. They touch us physically, mentally, emotionally, and spiritually. Even if we cannot hear auditory tones, we can still feel the vibrations sound waves produce.

Many research studies have shown the effects sound and music have on the human brain. Sound and music have long been a part of therapeutic modalities that help to ease pain and discomfort. Music makes us feel better. It calms us, shifts our mood, and energizes us. Cultures worldwide use music to connect to loved ones and mark special occasions. We play music at concerts, graduations, weddings, and birthdays, and we even sing lullabies to babies.

Hearing our favorite songs releases dopamine (the hormone responsible for making us happy), which activates our brain's pleasure centers. This energizes us and has an immediate, positive effect on our disposition. We can all relate to experiencing a mood boost as we belt out our favorite songs in the shower or car. We even connect music and sound to memories—a special song played on the radio, a school bell announcing the start of summer, or even a whistle from a kettle—these sounds offer us comfort and trigger fond memories.

Melodic tones played during distressing times can serve as a distraction, and some practitioners of healing modalities suggest that the simple vibratory effects of music itself are restorative. Percussive therapy, for example, uses vibratory massage tools to help improve muscle elasticity. Vibro-acoustic treatment (which is still under study), has shown promise in using sound vibrations for restorative purposes. Sound therapists, who use everything from crystal singing bowls to flutes, drums, chimes, and cymbals claim sound has numerous physical healing properties.

Therapists also use music to help patients with cognitive and neurological disorders and memory loss. Music helps such patients interact with others by stimulating an area of the brain called the supplementary motor cerebral cortex, where music memory is stored. It does not degrade as quickly with dementia or Alzheimer's the way other parts of the brain do. The online journal, *Neuroscience News*, reports that when patients with memory loss are exposed to music they enjoyed in the past, they become more alert cognitively, and can connect (temporarily) to family and loved ones with greater awareness.[7] Some can answer "Yes" and "No" questions and they can communicate socially. Music is meaningful at the bedside of dying patients as well. Because of its soothing effect, it can quiet patients and calm friends and families assisting a transitioning loved one. Music and sound can affect the neuroplasticity of the brain. Neuroplasticity is the brain's ability to form connections and reorganize functions that allow a person to learn and adapt after being subjected to stimuli. For example, neuroplasticity allows a person to recover from a stroke or seizure. Neuroplasticity is part of a normal, healthy brain as well. For example, every thought you have ever had formed a pathway in your brain. When a thought is reinforced or rewarded, it becomes engrained, and creates habits and responses to retained stimuli. Such responses are, of course, vital to our survival. However, our brains can also form new pathways and shut down old, deep-seated ones that no longer serve us. Neural pathways, part of the system that supports neuroplasticity, comprise chemical and electrical neurotransmitters, a series of neurons that are joined and send signals from one area

---

[7] Neuroscience News, "Long Term Musical Memory Spared in Alzheimer's Patients" (2015, June 19), https://neurosciencenews.com/musical-memory-alzheimers-2144/, Retrieved July 7, 2020.

of the brain to another. As we hear and feel music or sound, our neurons fire, sending information to certain areas of our brains. This stimulation allows us to feel joy, peace, and other emotions, as we connect to the music we are processing.

As noted earlier, our brains operate at different frequencies. Research suggests that the slower brain frequencies, Alpha, Theta, and Delta, support the brain's neuroplasticity to reform neural pathways. One way of achieving the calming effects of the lower brain waves is through music. Tones and beats help synchronize the brain to these lower frequencies rhythmically and induce a flow state, soothing anxiety, creating better memory recall, and connecting to intuitive guidance. A "flow state" occurs when we are engaged in an enjoyable activity. We lose track of time and are present and mindful. During this time, our brains release norepinephrine, anandamide, dopamine, serotonin, and endorphins. We feel productive, balanced, and have an overall sense of happiness. While these states occur naturally, sound can help induce them. Sound practitioners use a sound technology that offers "Binaural beats" and "Isochronic tones" to invoke these feel-good states.

Binaural beats are continuous tones emitted at two different frequencies delivered to each ear while a client is wearing headphones. These beats are between 4 Hz and 7 Hz and engage the Theta brain state. This aids in meditation practice and even sleep transition. Isochronic tones are similar. However, these tones are not constant. They are rhythmic and occur at regularly spaced intervals. Both methods help engage our lower brain waves, connecting us to our inner wisdom, soothing our busy minds, and increasing the neuroplasticity of our brains. Finding flow in our daily lives is imperative to our mental, emotional, and spiritual health. This is also true in elder care homes and hospices where patients can feel anxious, restless, or confused.

Patients with a cognitive disorder can experience restlessness or confusion that typically occurs in the late afternoon and evening. We call this "sundowning." Classical music and familiar sounds can help reduce sundowning symptoms and limit patient agitation. Playing classical music or exposing patients to familiar sounds stimulates the parts of the brain that are still functioning, bringing the active pathways to the forefront, promoting a sense of control and lucidity, and helping in memory recall. Music and sound can also reduce anxiety as dopamine and serotonin release.

As scientists conduct more scientific studies on the healing properties of sound, we discover that sound affects us more than we realize. Sound is within us. Our heartbeat, our breath, the very atoms that form us—all vibrate. These vibrations connect us to our reality. Intuitively recognizing the beneficial effects of sound helps establish entertaining, calming, and memorable moments in our lives.

The sound of creation is within each of you, the flow of your blood through your veins, the gentle thump of your heartbeat, the rushing of cells moving and dividing. There is deep knowledge of universal truth within you, for everything oscillates and vibrates on a frequency including what you deem your physical reality.
~ A-Team

Chapter 32

Mr. Ivan

When I was in training to become an End-of-Life Doula, I learned how important sound is in helping patients on their journeys toward death. I have always recognized the importance of music—how it is a universal language with the ability to bridge gaps between cultures around the world. Still, I had never paired it with death and dying. It seems obvious now, especially after learning that usually, hearing is the last of our five senses to fade.

Once I became certified in sound bowl therapy, I started using sound bowls with patients. During nursing home visits, I discovered many of the other residents wanted to take part in the sound bowl activities, too. Many had never played a sound bowl and were excited when I gave them a bowl, a wooden mallet, and free rein to experiment. Their eyes lit up with joy as they struck the bowl and a robust resonating sound reverberated outward. Others wanted to sit and listen as I glided the mallets around the rims of the bowls and struck the sides gently, filling the room with harmonizing sounds.

During these special days, I realized how important sound is. It brought shy residents out of their shells, calmed anger and bitterness in some people, brought life into the eyes of depressed patients, and brought joy and distraction to discontented people looking for a bit of hope. Taking part in the short musical moments created with the sound bowls softened the hearts of patients and other residents. Afterward, the patients who took part felt comfortable enough to open up to me about what they were going through—their fears, their pasts, and their concerns for the future. I was a more-than-willing listener and rarely had to say anything at all. Being present and allowing them to communicate verbally and through the music of the bowls allowed them to come to their own conclusions and decisions. It was as if all they needed to do was say out loud what their heads and hearts had kept pent up for so long. Sitting with them in a quiet, non-judgmental place was enough to bring out their inner wisdom. Music offered these patients more than just enjoyment. It provided a level of personal healing for all who gathered to listen and play.

I have used music and sound bowls at the bedsides of many patients, including Mr. Ivan. Long before immigrating to the United States from Russia, Mr. Ivan had been a music teacher and guitarist. His daughter told me he spoke fluent English, but aside from his love of watching TV with English subtitles, I never saw it. We communicated through charades. He smiled and spoke rarely, and replied to questions with small grunts and hard eye contact. At first, this felt unwelcoming and uncomfortable, but soon I learned he was rough around the edges and a man of few words.

On a hot summer afternoon, I stopped in to sit with my silent friend, and the television was not working. This was upsetting as he relied on it for distraction and entertainment. I had relied on the television to help pass the time too, as communication between us was strained. This day was going to be different. I played a game of charades with him, but it was almost one-sided. I considered calling it a day, but I knew he would be bored without me, regardless. *What could we do?* I excused myself and retrieved a sound bowl from the back seat of my car. When I returned, Mr. Ivan was still in the same spot. I placed the sound bowl and mallet in his lap. At first, he was not interested, but after I struck the bowl a few times, he gave it a go. He hit it timidly, but then his strikes became firm, loud, and resolute. It was not long before he tried to make distinct tones, but since it was only one bowl, he could only make one note.

Focused on the instrument, he forgot I was there. He played the bowl for several minutes before looking up, showing he was finished. I was amazed. It was the most engaged I had ever seen Mr. Ivan. To keep the momentum going, I played some music. I did not know what type of music he enjoyed, but I pulled out my phone and searched for a classical music playlist. Mozart's "Piano Sonata No. 16 in C Major" was the first piece to play.

After a few moments, my usual grouchy patient lifted his head. Then, I noticed his head swayed just a little, followed by his shoulders. His pointer finger started conducting the music ever so delicately. As the piece continued, his upper body moved in rhythm from his seated position as he anticipated each note. His eyes closed, as if he had been transported to an unseen world where pain and immobility were not an issue. His breath became deeper, fuller, less shallow. The music brought him to life. The next piece that played was Beethoven's "Für Elise," and his enthusiasm continued. I am grateful to have reached my patient in a new way. The language of music, the symphony of sound, had us both enjoying our time together in a way we had never done before.

As our private concert ended, a minor miracle happened. Mr. Ivan graced me with a closed-lip smile. I could not help but applaud—a breakthrough. Our sessions after that contained a classical musical interlude and what felt like a genuine appreciation for our time together.

As Mr. Ivan's last days grew closer, he became withdrawn. I tried to comfort him, but Mr. Ivan shifted inward as death approached. On the day he took his last breath, I was sitting bedside. I held his feet as his family surrounded him, holding his hands and touching his head gently. I played his favorite classical music pieces until his final exhale. His last breath was peaceful, and the family felt both sadness and relief as they said goodbye to Mr. Ivan.

A couple of days later, I was thinking of Mr. Ivan and grieving for my transitioned friend. My phone, which was in my purse, started playing the classical playlist I had made for him. It was perfect timing. As the music played, I felt grateful. It was a beautiful encore. Thank you, Mr. Ivan. Bravo.

Your universe serenades, singing sublimely from the heavens. You cannot hear with your ears as it hums in harmony with the stars. The symphony ripples a cosmic chant felt in the Soul, all in perfect time.

~ A-Team

Chapter 33

The Takeaway – Go Within

One of the most important things we can do for ourselves and our planet is to go within and silence our minds. Quieting the mind is the path to balance, inspiration, and clarity. It is the way to connect to one's true Self and to take time away from the distractions of our material world. Inside of each of us is a wealth of knowledge, ideas, and concepts, just waiting for us to tap into it. As we navigate the complexities of our modern world, seeking to find peace and clarity in our busy lives, we can find the tranquility we seek within ourselves.

When we meditate intending to connect to something greater than ourselves, we shift our focus from our physical reality to our inner awareness. We listen for that still, small voice within us. Often, our inner voice sounds like our thoughts, but there is a subtle difference. The words or images that pop into our minds will always be kind, non-judgmental, and wise. They may seem like our imagination at first, but with practice comes discernment.

At the beginning of your meditation journey, it is important to journal your experience as the information received can be tough to recall later on. Also, reviewing your notes can be handy as you realize the accuracy and helpfulness of the information that came through. It builds trust in your inner voice and fosters an openness to Spirit.

Before I meditate, often I say a prayer or set my intention for the answers I seek. Other times, I wait to hear what A-Team wants to share. Even with daily practice, I still ask myself things like, "Did I start the dishwasher?" or "Do I have all the ingredients for dinner tonight?" It is common to think mundane thoughts during meditation.

As Souls focused on this stream of reality, our minds wander to the physical life we are creating for ourselves. It is important to recognize this chatter as part of the process. Do not give up. When random thoughts arise in your mind, recenter your focus inward once more, and practice listening for your inner, spiritual voice again.

We are Spirit expressing ourselves through our physical form. The experience we choose here on this planet and the responsibilities and connections we make are an intricate element of this part of our Soul's purpose and growth. Our life and the details it comprises are part of the depth and richness of our Soul's participation here. Our physical experiences (like jet skiing, buying a boat, wrecking a car, stubbing a toe, eating a sweet treat, or giving a hug,) lend to our overall exposure to emotional stimuli, and promotion of pain, joy and a variety of other feelings. But it is also imperative to turn inward, to set aside our material world, and to remember that we are more than just this one personality having this one physical life. When we set our distractions aside and connect to ourselves and something greater, we find balance. We get to know ourselves and our true nature—not just who we are as we relate to our physical environment. We are so much more than that.

While meditating to quiet our minds, attain peace, or connect to Source is vital to understanding ourselves, it is just as important to apply the knowledge we gain in meditation to our physical lives. The insight that comes to us in meditation improves our existence and the lives of those around us.

When we establish a long-term meditation practice, we recognize that while we are all individual personalities, we are also all One in Spirit. We gain a greater understanding of how we have developed our relationships with ourselves and those around us based on long-held (perhaps even taught-to-us) belief systems. By releasing those limiting beliefs, we can strengthen our relationships with others and ourselves. Through meditation, we open our hearts, appreciating how beautiful and complex each of us is and understanding that we are all flowing within our Soul's potential. A-Team says, "You are potential." Potential energy, scientifically speaking, is the energy held by an object relative to other objects. A-Team explains that each of us *is* potential. We are the energy stored in our material selves. We can create and we can alter other objects around us. We are creating and ready to go in every moment. We are potential.

A-Team explained to me that stillness allows for clarity when we are seeking our true self:

> *My friend, Truth is a big word. It holds much. Like a glass of water, your true self is the glass, the vessel of who you are. It contains the pure water of your personality. Experiences, taught beliefs, untrue thoughts, and history, as defined by your world, agitate, and muddy the waters of your personality, hiding the true self. But the Truth of who you are is always there, supporting, surrounding, and holding you. When one takes time to sit in solitude, to find the stillness within, the tumultuous muddy waters slow. The sediment settles, and the clear waters of the personality become evident. The Truth of oneself becomes distinguishable once more. One recognizes the sediment that has settled at the bottom of the glass is now a bed of experiences and challenges one has risen above.*

A-Team's imagery of the continuous chaos, thoughts, beliefs, and history swirling around us helps us to visualize the limiting ideologies in which we invest. When we take time to still our minds and allow a peaceful awareness of our true selves to emerge, an alternative, open-minded, and flexible approach to our physical lives reveals itself. We consider alternative perspectives, allowing inspiration to flow. A greater understanding of ourselves emerges. This leads to a greater understanding of others and increases our ability to connect in loving, peaceful ways to the world in which we live and create.

Reflecting and turning inward to connect is also possible through creativity. I do this through painting or cultivating plants. Although creating something new sometimes puts us in a thinking mindset, letting go of preconceived ideas and creating is an excellent way to blend into the flow of our Spirit. Our unique brand of creativity raises appreciation for beauty in the world. Expressing gratitude for our creations, as perfectly imperfect as they may be, reminds us of the perfectly imperfect world we live in.

Another way to connect to something greater than ourselves is by observing nature.

Whether we are watching the brilliant colors play in the sky as the sun sets, feeling a breeze caress our skin, admiring the majesty of a mighty oak, or listening to birds singing, tuning in with an open heart to our glorious world connects us to the knowledge that life is good. We are safe to be still in the now. At these moments, we feel balanced, connected, and inspired.

Hello, Little Sprout. Inspiration floats like seeds on the surrounding breeze. Perhaps you will slow down enough to see it, catch it, or even cultivate it. Follow your heart. Love, trust, let's see what grows. New worlds spring up from tiny seeds of inspiration.
~ A-Team

Part III

Questions and Answers

Chapter 34

Frequently Asked Questions

In my work as an intuitive advisor, teacher, and Death Doula, often I engage in spiritual and philosophical conversations with patients and their families. Patients ask deep questions like *What should I expect in the process of death? What happens after we die? What is the meaning of life? Who are we? Why are we here? What is our purpose? Is there a God?* I have thought about these questions and asked A-Team to share their insight about our universe and what it means to experience the human condition. To help readers understand these profound topics, I am sharing some of the most common questions my clients and their families ask. I gleaned the answers below from consultations with A-Team and in meditation from my Higher Self. I hope they help you navigate the challenges and gifts of your life in earthly form.

What is consciousness?

Consciousness is a state of being aware. According to A-Team, consciousness is a state in which we exist, a form of Being. It is everything we experience, from our physical senses to our thoughts. Yes, even inanimate, imagined things are conscious. Everything is experiencing. Everything has its state of consciousness, right down to every atom and particle. Everything is Source expressing itself. You, me, and everything in our world are all conscious on some level. A-Team once answered my questions about consciousness like this:

Feel the sun on your face. That is love. Yes, every molecule has consciousness derived from love, from Source. That particle followed its path, its direction in its life to serve by helping to supply warmth and light for other life on your planet to thrive and benefit. Every particle, every life has a purpose, a direction, and all the particles that make you up are no different, for they are the same. You, too, have a purpose, a path, a direction; all the particles and molecules that make up every part of what you call "you" support you, your consciousness. But they are consciousness, too. They help you and you support them. It's symbiotic. It's connection. There can be no other way.

Is there a God? Who or What is God?

I get asked this question a lot. I describe my thoughts on God like this: What God is not is a man sitting on a throne in the sky, judging human beings' choices. *God is.* God is All That Is. God is Love. God is Source, Creator, and Creation. Every single thing, animate or inanimate, is God. Every molecule, atom, particle, and ion is God. God, Source, All That Is, is Divinity's most genuine and authentic form. When we align ourselves with truth and Love, we can feel God. When a greater, Godly awareness enters our thoughts, we feel joy. We are God experiencing itself in infinite ways.

Are there angels?

For a long time, I have hesitated to commit to the word "angel" because it holds so many religious and cultural connotations. Sometimes I feel labeling something confines it to a box, limiting it instead of helping others relate to and understand it. But my many experiences with angelic beings leave me with no other vocabulary to express my encounters. So, yes, there are angels.

Angels feel different from the connection I have to deceased loved ones. The feeling is more encompassing and protective. It leaves me awestruck. The angels are loving, powerful, and commanded respect. One angel encounter I had happened one evening visiting a friend's house. I noticed two angels in her living room. They radiated bright white light, and one was holding a trumpet. They were as tall as the ceiling, but I knew that if they had been in a larger room with a higher ceiling, they would have filled that space, too. The confines of the room did not apply to their reality.

As I focused on the two beings, they told me they were there to support my friend's sons, Conner and Jackson. The one on the left was Archangel Gabriel, and he showed me how he holds Conner's hand during his nightly sleep travels. Gabriel gave me an overwhelming sense of friendship between the two of them—he did not feel superior to Conner—and I knew that, at heart, Conner is a teacher.

The second Angel glowed in beautiful, rich shades of blue, and carried a sword and shield. I recognized him as Archangel Michael. He walked toward the hallway to Jackson's room. As he moved, I saw his feet up close. He was wearing what looked to be gladiator sandals. Michael gave me the feeling he was there to protect Jackson through an experience he would have in the future. Michael's role in Jackson's life was to help Jackson voice his truth and speak up for his beliefs, tapping into his courage and strength.

While angels and archangels can visit human beings and assist us with handling life's trials and tribulations, some people question how angels know how to help us if they themselves (as some mediums say) have never had physical incarnations. It has been my experience that Spirit in all forms is limitless. When I ask A-Team, they agree Spirit is Limitless and that angelic beings can be physical if they need to be. We are all One, part of the greater whole, part of All That Is. If an entity wants to experience life and take part as a human being, we would be arrogant to assume that only "we" get to be human and those experiencing existence at a frequency of an angelic being are not "allowed" to experience life in a physical form.

Is there a heaven?

Yes. Heaven is the home of our Souls and the place we return to between incarnations and chosen experiences. It is both our starting point and our destination. Many words describe heaven, including, "the other side," "across the veil," "paradise," and even the "flip side." Heaven is not a place in the clouds filled with harps and pearly gates. According to A-Team, it is home to our eternal Self. Heaven is creation. It is permanent, just as we are. Ideas, concepts, and chosen experiences are often worked out here first, by our Higher Selves and then acted out in our physical worlds. While heaven may not be physical, per se, items in heaven appear physical to beings who live there because the frequency of the objects and the beings' match. Like here, the frequency of our bodies and the material world match. If a person in Spirit were to visit Earth, things here on Earth would not seem physical to them because their frequency or vibration of molecules is vibrating differently than our earthly molecules. Likewise, we are unaware of the items on the other side because we are not vibrating at the same frequency as beings there are. Everything is here, but since everything is vibrating at different levels, different Beings experience it in different ways.

Is there a hell?

No, not really. I have never had a Soul validate hell yet. In fact, they have expressed the opposite. I have had Spirit say that Souls who choose to take part in a challenging, hellish experience can do so if they feel it is something they need to do. We have seen this in some people's accounts of their Near-Death Experiences (NDE's). But their experience is brief. It is not an eternal damnation. The only everlasting experience of the Spirit is one of Love, creation, acceptance, and growth for the sake of experiencing. We are Source experiencing itself, as itself, in countless ways.

Will I be forgiven for my sins?

Forgiveness is something you must give yourself. God does not judge you for your actions, so there is no requirement that others forgive you. However, Spirit people come through mediums and ask for forgiveness from a surviving loved one because of their actions while they were in physical form. Spirits do this as a way of taking responsibility for their actions. They are now more aware than ever how their actions affected others, and able to see a bigger picture of how their choices caused fear, pain, or suffering. Spirits ask for forgiveness because it is a way of taking responsibility, and it is helpful for the surviving loved ones because it facilitates the removal of guilt, shame, or anger the loved one may internalize because of the deceased's behavior in life. Asking for forgiveness is a kind act for the one who is suffering. It starts the healing process, and new experiences and realizations can grow. This teaches empathy and encourages the practice of it in other physical situations. It allows the loved one still on Earth to move forward and keep their thoughts from spiraling into the past or blaming the deceased loved one for their continued hurt.

How will I be judged for my sins?

There is not judgment in the way we understand it here on Earth. No one judges us for our choices or punishes us for our wrongs. There is not "good" or "bad" in the way we deem them to be in our earthly laws and rules. Every act considered "good" or "bad" is an opportunity for a Soul's growth for the sake of experiencing. There is wisdom in every action, every choice, and every thought. Sins or immoral acts deemed to be transgressions against God are not judged or punished. There is always cause and effect from our choices. We have free will, but eternal punishment is not the outcome of our choices. Acts deemed immoral have changed throughout history and cultures. For example, an action justified in one area of the globe at another time in history may be seen as wrong or unethical now. We can justify sinful acts and we can rationalize acts of complacency. These are ethical considerations that facilitate a greater level of awareness and growth on a Soul level.

Each "death" experience is unique, but it is my understanding that at some point, the deceased realizes how their actions in life—all their inspiration, kindness, hope, anger, resentment, and pain—rippled out and affected those around them. All our choices have an effect, and those choices color how we experience ourselves while manifesting in a material form. We are the only ones who judge us. We judge ourselves. Free will rules All That Is, both in physical form and not. We consider what we want to experience and co-create that experience to facilitate our wants and needs.

If we are not judged, then what about "evil" people and acts?

This is a sensitive topic and difficult to discuss because people hold deep-rooted beliefs about what evil is. It has been my experience so far that evil is simply a concept. It is an act that one perceives as causing intentional harm or suffering. Any action is neutral until one assigns an emotion or a belief to it. It is only destructive if we perceive it as hurtful. Evil is a thought form, a perspective, and ignorance all at the same time. A thought form is a projection of mental energy or a pattern a person creates. These are ideas, concepts, feelings, and emotions. We cannot see thought forms with our physical eyes, but many people can perceive them energetically. Thoughts are things. They exist in a distinct reality than we experience materially.

We have all heard the adage that "hurt people hurt people," which is true. Where a person has internalized their pain and suffering, there is a need to lash out, blame, or hurt someone else for the injustice to which others have subjected them. Are they evil for being victimized? No. They are hurting and expressing outwardly what they feel they lack inwardly. Are they evil for victimizing another because of their hurt? No, they are not evil. Understanding the intent behind one's actions is crucial. Knowing one's inner truth of hurt and suffering and recognizing where it stems from is the first step to greater understanding. Taking responsibility for your actions brings a greater awareness and understanding of Self and the feelings of others and it inspires compassion and love.

As a follow-up question, I often hear, "Then what about the greatest transgression of all, the taking of a life through suicide or murder?"

This is a hard question to answer because I do not condone such behavior. However, Spirit has weighed in on this and I must share. I will start by addressing the concept of suicide. I have had many Spirits show up in readings who transitioned by completing suicide. They come across just as beautiful, loving, and vibrant as any other Soul whose death occurred because of natural causes or accidental circumstances.

I have never experienced a Soul who is "stuck" or "trapped" or unable to "move on peacefully" because they transitioned by their own hand. However, often they come through with an apology for how their suicide affected surviving loved ones. Sometimes, they ask for forgiveness to ease the guilt surviving family and friends may have surrounding their untimely death. They take responsibility for the hurt, pain, and shame their suicide caused others. They suggest they could not see their own value and worth in the world and, as a result, decided leaving was the best choice. Sometimes they say their suicide resulted from a chemical imbalance or a defect in their physical makeup that supported the emotional spiral that led to their death. Occasionally, they express that once they transitioned, they realized their choice to die was not the best option, and now they know how loved they were. They could not see the bigger picture. At other times, Spirit suggests some suicides are unavoidable or fell within that Soul's "exit window" or time frame of death. If not suicide, then another way of dying would have been on the horizon.

With murder, survivors undergo a deep wound of loss, injustice, anger, and fear. The death of any loved one is difficult, but death by murder leaves loved ones paralyzed with questions surrounding the violent transition. In my experience, when a murdered Spirit comes through, they still come in a beautiful light and vibrancy. They are not angry, seeking justice, or unable to move on until they somehow avenge their death. They come through understanding that their death is a great experience for growth, not just for their loved ones, but often, on a grander scale, rippling far out into the community and, sometimes, globally. Their death brings awareness to central issues such as mental health, lack of widespread connections and compassion through injustice, and social and environmental concerns, to name a few. Often, they view their deaths from a positive perspective, recognizing how their death served a greater whole. For us left behind, seeing the positive in a loved one's death can be difficult to relate to and hard to accept. Also, they are aware of the unfathomable pain their loved ones feel for their loss, and instead of explaining why they transitioned in the manner they did, they focus on sending messages of love to their family and friends, letting them know they are safe and okay, and they are not gone. They reiterate how they still hear and feel their surviving loved ones and work to send them moments of peace and love. They hope that their loved ones find peace and continue to live their lives to the fullest, rather than holding themselves back in feelings of guilt, unfairness, or fear that their joy in life somehow dishonors the deceased.

Often, surviving families question if their murdered loved one felt pain or fear in their last moments. Spirit assures me that in moments when the Soul does not want or need to experience such trauma, the consciousness separates itself from the body in the last moments and experiences the situation outside the physical body. While the physical body goes through the violent process of shutting down and even struggles to survive, the consciousness of the individual is safe and is observing the unfolding events on a different level. I have also heard that, sometimes, Spirits have forgotten the trauma around their transition but are aware of how it occurred. I liken this to a mother forgetting the traumas around a difficult childbirth. Looking back, she knows it was hard and painful but does not quite remember the pain or her fear.

Suicide and murder are painful human experiences that leave gaping emotional wounds in surviving families and communities. Still, Spirits assert that life is eternal, and we are always safe and loved.

Will I suffer at death? Will it be painful?

It has been my experience through many bedside visitations that at the time of death, the Soul of the dying person is often outside their physical body. The Soul (who we are) is already experiencing great freedom, expansiveness, and peace. While the dying person's physical body appears to struggle or suffer, the actual person is not experiencing that. Death itself is not usually painful, but freeing. Spirit has expressed that dying is straightforward and that we should not confuse the physical body's shutting down with a fearful, scary, or painful experience for the Soul. Spirit has told me this is almost always the case, unless the Soul wanted or needed to experience their death, including the struggle or pain. I have been told this is not common but, of course, it is an option on a Soul level. (I expressed this in the Mrs. Wilma chapter.)

Will my loved ones always greet me at death?

Absolutely. At each client death for which I have been present, Spirit tells me about or shows me a waiting room, a gathering, or a party of Souls waiting to greet their loved one. The feeling is one of great excitement, joy, and anticipation. While we are experiencing grief and a sense of loss on this side, the loved ones in heaven are joyous to be reunited with their loved ones. When a Soul transitions before any of their close loved ones do, their team of guides, angels, and loved ones they know on the other side (even those they never knew in their recent physical life) greet them.

Will I be ready to die?

This is a personal question, but Spirit assures me that a Soul transitions when they, on a Soul level, have agreed to it. At the very least, there is a probability of things unfolding in this way. I like the analogy I have heard others share about so called "exit points." It is as if life in our physical reality is like traveling on a freeway, and we may take certain exits. Maybe we take them; maybe we do not. Maybe we plan on taking one exit, but through free will or the free will of another, we miss that exit and realign ourselves for the next one. My guides tell me we often work this out before the event occurs. Other Souls may not need exit points, and they decide in advance on a Soul level that they will die at a specific time. And so it is. Either way, most people realize (even if on some subconscious level) that they will transition, and the Soul prepares itself in the best manner to make the departure as smooth as possible.

What if I don't want to die?

This is sometimes the case in people who receive a diagnosis of a terminal illness. They have the wind knocked out of their sails and feel they are leaving too soon. They are not ready. This is where the work of a doula can be helpful. Death doulas help people by bringing awareness and peace to the unavoidable. This makes the transition smoother and fills it with love and hope. There is closure. When a person is open to the work, they find acceptance as the end grows closer.

Is there life after death?

Of course, Spirit says we only have *one* life; but we have many multi-dimensional experiences.

Does my life have purpose/meaning?

Of course. You may not feel your life is making a difference here on earth, but Spirit assures me that every life is an integral part of the greater whole—as depicted in Mrs. Wilma's story. Although you may not feel your life is adding up in importance, it is. Your actions contribute to your experiences for your Higher Self and to the knowledge, understanding, and wisdom of those you meet and with whom you interact. Some people have the limiting idea that one life is better than another based on age, rank, financial standing, power, family name, or title. But in Heaven, we are all the same. Every life is of equal value, and no amount of earthly successes, challenges overcome, or choices made will change the relative value of a single Soul.

What does it feel like to make a Spirit connection?

The feeling is subtle. There are many ways to connect—meditation, chanting, yoga, shamanistic journeying, etc. Every person has a unique method of connecting with Spirit, and Spirit has unique ways of connecting with every person. It is always fun, for example, when Spirit impresses song lyrics on me. In one situation with a client, I heard the Bob Dylan song, "All Along the Watchtower."[8] The song was popular before my time, but I had heard it before. When I googled it, I discovered that Bob Dylan wrote it, and Jimi Hendrix covered it. The song is about changing or going against established social norms in favor of a new or different set of values. I also heard

---

[8] Bob Dylan, "All Along the Watchtower," John Wesley Harding, 1967, Produced by Bob Johnston, Columbia Records.

that the name of the deceased loved one in Spirit correlated to the song's artists. Both notions applied to my client. Her ex-husband was coming through, and his name was Robert "Bob" James. (Hendrix's birth name was Johnny Allen Hendrix; his family later changed it to James Marshall Hendrix. "Jimi" is a nickname for James). My client's deceased loved one was named after both artists! Also, my client had left her husband at a point in societal history when divorce was not okay. She went against the established social norms to create new sets of values for her children. The song itself and the artists who recorded it were highly relevant.

Isn't it easier in heaven than it is here on Earth?

Yes and no. Jacob, one of my guides on A-Team, told me, "Everyone there thinks it's easier here. It's different. I suppose some things are easier by your standards, but I assure you it is more challenging in other ways. The work you do is vital, of course, not to diminish it. You are given slack because you are limited by choice. I am granted less so." I suppose there are always challenges to some degree on this side and the other side... but we continue to learn and grow through them.

I'm spiritual but my partner is not. I don't feel supported in my beliefs. How can I find peace with my partner?

I hear this all the time. There was a time when the difference in belief systems between me and Taylor bothered me. Spirit shared some words of wisdom that helped me feel safe and understanding. "He doesn't want to wake up yet. He's sleeping in! That's okay, right? You've always been an early bird. He's a night owl. Everyone wakes up in their own time. There is no rush—only love. Please don't force it. That's not pleasant for anyone or necessary. It matters not. Let it be. He is loved, same as you. Not less, not more."

Taylor may not feel completely comfortable discussing what happens after death and he isn't a meditator either. But I have come to see that his connection to All That Is expresses through his photography and appreciation of sunsets. It's how he connects to himself, others and to creation as a whole. That is Divine, just from a different lens than what I am using.

Is Déjà vu a spiritual sign?

This is an interesting question, as many of us have Déjà vu experiences regularly. But to answer this question, I turned to A-Team. A-Team said:

Before you came into this physical existence, you, as a greater Soul, knew you wanted to experience certain aspects of physical life. You worked with other greater Souls to plan what such a life would look like in many degrees. Of course, you are already a life, but we speak of physical existence within a set of parameters. It's a complicated process done with seriousness but also in joy. Just like in your earthly forms, there are energies/Souls toward whom you gravitate. You choose to create an existence with them for the fun of it! Then you all meet together and create a storyline and characters, if you will, that complement each greater Soul's needs, wants, and desires. Each role varies, but the intent is to act out such lives to accommodate each greater Soul's experiences. Lives are not created to bring suffering, but each Soul knows that lives or experiences chosen with limited, boxed-in parameters or belief systems will probably cause suffering, pain, and hurt because of the feelings of lack, loss, and disconnection that one existence of limitation often brings. But, the knowledge and wisdom gained from such experiences and the joys in each life, as you know it, outweigh, in most circumstances, the suffering. The Soul knows it is always safe, always connected, and it can be no other way. Life, like a roller coaster, has a lot of ups and downs. There's a lot of anticipation, excitement, and nervousness before one starts the ride, followed by mixed emotions while on the ride and then relief when the ride is over. In your physical lives (a blink/flicker image appears in my mind's eye), your personality reconnects with your greater Self /Soul many times a day without you even being aware of this. There is an exchange/download of expected plans and choices one personality may choose to make with their own free will. This includes all decisions from the significant and life-altering to the mundane daily chores. Sometimes, when the personality tunes in to this download of these plans and acts them out, they have a "I have I done this before" effect. Déjà vu, my friend, yes, and in some ways, you have. You relayed your goals to your greater self, and Voila, tu as bu la fontaine, mon amour (you drank from the fountain, my love). You connected and tuned in to yourself, your Higher Self. Take it as a clue that you are connected, you are not alone, and you are on the path selected by you for you and for the highest good of those you are working with. This does not mean a particular déjà vu moment is noteworthy per se, it is just that you were connected and right where you were supposed to be where you chose to be. There is more to say here, but for now, this should suffice.

Open your mind to more expansive thoughts, young one, for it's challenging to grasp the concepts if you have a limited mind/belief system. To live a singular life over and over would be uneventful and tedious. Such experiences of life are not so. With that being said, there are opportunities after one leaves a physical body to explore choices/decisions from a different point of view. Paths not taken are still played out and recorded, even if you are unaware of this. If one should choose, they may explore these paths and insert them into their "timeline" or "event loop." Personalities wanting to get it perfect do this. You would call them "Type A." This, of course, is an exercise for the personalities wanting to "get it right." It isn't a "do-over" because the personalities who created the other players of each life scenario are no longer present. Similar to editing a film, the players/characters are all there, but the personalities are not. Therefore, you live your life (or experience) as one personality once, but the experiences remain like a story on a screen to be experienced by all who wish to. It is a part of who you are on a larger scale, a larger Soul. Each life experience or personality is part of a fragment of a larger Soul, being, or entity. You, as you know yourself, are only a part of who you are. All the various selves that have been creating and acting out experiences for you bring you knowledge and awareness and help you perfect yourself. You are a greater Soul. Déjà vu, my friend. What fun! What a gift. You are fortunate to have such a clue.

Where and how do our life experiences remain after we die?

This is an interesting question. A record of our lives, deeds, actions, and thoughts remain in a form accessible by your Higher Self and others. There are many names for these records: Akashic Records, Hall of Memories, Book of Life, Hall of Journals, Book of Remembrance, and others. Regardless of the term used, they are a vast, energetic accumulation of all universal events that transcend all dimensions and planes of existence. The records hold information, thoughts, emotions, intentions, insight, wisdom, and the teachings of everyone. Some people while in their physical earthly lives can gain information from these records which help them better understand who they are on a Higher Self level. Often, learning of our experiences or other lives gives us the strength to endure challenges in this life, as we remember our challenges in other incarnations. Accessing this information helps us remember we are not just our one personality, and we can see a new perspective: we are so much more than this one life.

When Spirit has shown me these records, they have depicted them as a great library that holds books, computer-like databases, movies, meeting rooms, theaters, gathering spaces, and common areas, and it appears to be built from white marble that emanates light. The dome-ceiling flows with wavy patterns of pink, blue, and purple light. When I ask questions about my other incarnations or the purpose of my current life, a being of light escorts me to a book stand where a giant book about the size of a backpack rests. The book opens, seemingly intuitively, to the page that holds the information I am seeking. While there, I witness other people accessing their information and sometimes Spirit beings lead them into a screening room where a movie plays. I imagine how one receives the information is personal and unique, varying by personality.

Who, what, where, when, and why am I?

Who am I? I am. I am experiencing all parts of myself by allowing myself to connect to others and try out lives with varying circumstances and choices. For myself, I am a personality here called Gretchen, but I am also a much bigger Soul experiencing itself through various personalities in various dimensions or worlds. I am.

What am I?

I am a Soul who is always safe, free, not bound by limitations or expectations, and who is Love. I am aware, and through experience, lessons, and teachings in various circumstances and opportunities, I am a student and teacher realizing myself both in form and not in form simultaneously.

Where am I?

I am right here, right now, not confined by the limitations of time and space. But occasionally, I choose to experience a linear existence for the sake of learning, connecting, and trying new things. It is fun, and I am grateful to be here.

When am I?

Now. I am in the present moment. I am imbued with the self-awareness to recognize I am here, NOW. Every moment is now. When am I? I am Now.

Why am I?

I am an aspect of the Creator, an aspect of Self, an aspect of All That Is. As awareness, I experience myself in as many ways as possible through various density levels, choices, opportunities, and more. In doing so, I create and co-create personalities and worlds, all for the sake of experiencing and knowing myself more fully in awareness. I am a magnificent creator who experiences life because I want to. There is an expansion in my knowledge of Self. I create new things and experiences constantly, for the joy of it. Knowing I am safe on a higher level (on a Soul level instead of on a personality level) encourages my Soul to experience hardships that are also divine. I *get* to do this. I do it to explore, learn, and know myself more through varying experiences as I recognize the truth of my many diverse selves (fragments of various personalities).

Have a look around you. Life is made up of building blocks, of layers, of small teams, creating and making up larger units, everything linked, everything connected. Everything's part of a greater whole/system/reality. Different intensity levels back your feelings and emotions. When you speak of your love/joy/excitement or your hurt/resentment/anger, those emotions are charged and create thought forms. Be mindful of your thoughts and trust that all unfolds in divine timing.
~ A-Team

I am incredibly grateful for A-Team and I cannot imagine my existence without them. They continue to be a source of unconditional love, deep wisdom, humor, joy, and compassionate understanding. They encouraged me to write a book, one that communicates the importance of what I know and what I have learned so far through my personal experiences. I wrote about my work as a Death Doula and an intuitive advisor and about my relationship with my guides. I hope that after reading this book you will realize there is so much more going on in the world that we do not perceive with our physical eyes. With a little practice and intention, you too can have access to this great wisdom and Love. You are never alone. Life is eternal. We all are a part of a spiritual team that is also a part of a greater Oneness through Source.

Meet Gretchen

Helen Gretchen Jones is a compassionate death doula, intuitive, and channeler who writes about shared death experiences and the essence of spiritual consciousness. Her writing focuses on fostering loving connections with oneself and others, and her work emphasizes trusting personal experiences and the teachings she channels from her team in Spirit, known as the A-Team.

Helen holds a dual master's degree in art history and theology from St. Edward's University. She is also certified in sound bowl therapy, Reiki, hypnosis, and past life regressions. Beyond her role as a death doula, Helen serves as an intuitive guide, delivering messages from Spirit. She co-teaches seminars with her community ranging from grounding techniques to interpreting messages and signs from Spirit, enriching the lives of diverse women across central Texas.

When she's not working with hospice patients, writing, or teaching, Helen can be found on the family ranch hanging out with her husband, Taylor, their children, Ty and Ellie, and their menagerie of animals, including birds, cats, llamas, and goats.

A Note To The Reader

I want to express my deepest gratitude to each of you for joining me on this incredible journey through the pages of *Healing Whispers from Spirit Guides*. Your decision to explore the depths of spirituality, life, and death alongside me means the world. To deepen your spiritual connection, I invite you to continue your journey with me. Join my empowering seminars and workshops, download my book club questions, and explore more on my website at **HelenGretchenJones.com**. For regular inspiration and updates, connect with me on social media **@HelenGretchenJones**.

Thank you for embracing this journey with an open heart and mind. I am truly honored to have you by my side as we delve into the mysteries of the soul and the wisdom of the spirit world.

Helen

Bibliography

"Astral Projection." Wikipedia, 2023. *Wikimedia Foundation.* Last modified April 16, 2024. https://en.wikipedia.org/wiki/Astral_projection.

Berliner, Phil. "Flow at Work: How to Boost Engagement in the Workplace." *YouTube*, 1 Feb. 2023. Accessed 7 Jul. 2023.

Black Pumas. "Colors." *Black Pumas.* Virgin Music, 2019. Produced by Adiran Quesada. Recorded in Deluxe Recorders in Austin.

Bottom Science (2019, January 1). "Dirac's Hole Theory Explained." Retrieved June 6, 2020, from https://www.bottomscience.com/diracs-hole-theory-explained/.

CERN (2021, March 21). "The Story of Antimatter." Retrieved July 7, 2021, from https://timeline.web.cern.ch/timeline-header/86#415.

CERN. (2012, January 1). "Higgs Boson." Retrieved November 7, 2020, from https://home.cern/science/physics/higgs-boson.

Dignity Memorial. (September 26, 2015). "Dr. Kurt Gabriel Hofer." Retrieved June 6, 2020, from https://www.dignitymemorial.com/obituaries/tallahassee-fl/kurt-hofer-6604384.

Dirac Sea. (2023, October 25). *Wikipedia.* https://en.wikipedia.org/wiki/Dirac_sea.

Dirac, Paul. (2023, August 30). *Wikipedia*. https://en.wikipedia.org/wiki/Paul_Dirac.

"Double Slit Experiment." (2023, October 27). *Wikipedia*. https://en.wikipedia.org/wiki/Double-slit_experiment.

Dylan, Bob. "All Along the Watchtower." *John Wesley Harding*, 1967. Produced by Bob Johnston, Columbia Records.

Farmelo, G. (2008, September 23). "Paul Dirac: The Mozart of Science." *Institute for Advanced Study*. Retrieved June 16, 2020, from https://www.ias.edu/ideas/2008/farmelo-on-dirac.

Fields, R. Douglas. "The Power of Music: Mind Control by Rhythmic Sound." *Scientific American*, 19 Jan. 2012, https://blogs.scientificamerican.com/guest-blog/the-power-of-music-mind-control-by-rhythmic-sound/#:~:text=The%20EEG%20recordings%20showed%20that,beat%20in%20the%20drum%20rhythm. Accessed 11 Nov. 2023.

Fink, Jennifer. "Why—And How—Music Moves Us." *Pfizer*, 1 Jan. 2008, www.pfizer.com/news/articles/why_and_how_music_moves_us#:~:text=Listening%20to%20(or%20making)%20music,that%20generate%20and%20control%20emotions.&text=The%20limbic%20system%2C%20which%20is,when%20our%20ears%20perceive%20music. Accessed 11 Nov. 2023.

Florida State University (1999, December 24). "Newton's Prism Experiments." *Molecular Expressions, Science Optics and You*. Retrieved July 7, 2020, from https://micro.magnet.fsu.edu/primer/java/scienceopticsu/newton/.

Galilei, Galileo. (2023, October 20). *Wikipedia*. https://en.wikipedia.org/wiki/Galileo_Galilei.

Paul Dirac. (2024, April 16). Wikipedia. https://en.wikipedia.org/wiki/Paul_Dirac.

Kassia. (2021, March 23). *Beethoven's Symphony #5* [Video]. YouTube. https://www.youtube.com/watch?v=8QorZ9fcg3o.

Edwards, Luke. (March 1 2023). "Designing 'The Dark Side of the Moon': Behind Pink Floyd's Iconic Album Cover." Designed by Storm Thorgerson, Illustrated by George Hardie. https://thisisdig-com-clone.nds.acquia-psi.com/feature/pink-floyd-the-dark-side-of-the-moon-album-cover-story/.

"LIGO-Virgo-KAGRA Finds Elusive Mergers of Black Holes with Neutron Stars." *LIGO Laser Interferometer Gravitational-Wave Observatory Supported by the National Science Foundation Operated by Caltech and MIT.* (2021, June 29). Retrieved July 7, 2021, from https://www.ligo.caltech.edu/news/ligo20210629.

Lin, T. (2019, May 14). "How Feynman Diagrams Revolutionized Physics." *Quanta Magazine.* Retrieved June 8, 2020, from https://www.quantamagazine.org/how-feynman-diagrams-revolutionized-physics-20190514/.

Little Miss Sunshine. (2023, September 17). Directed by Jonathan Dayton and Valerie Faris. From a screenplay written by Michael Arndt. Cast: Greg Kinnear, Steve Carell, Toni Collette, Paul Dano, Abigail Breslin, and Alan Arkin. In *Wikipedia.* https://en.wikipedia.org/wiki/Little_Miss_Sunshine.

"Marie Curie." Wikipedia, 2023. *Wikimedia Foundation.* Last modified October 16, 2023. https://en.wikipedia.org/wiki/Marie_Curie.

Mercury, Freddie. "Bohemian Rhapsody." *A Night at the Opera.* EMI. Roy Thomas Baker, Producer. Queen, Producer. Rockfield Studio, et al., London, 1975.

https://en.wikipedia.org/wiki/Bohemian_Rhapsody.

Mohandas E. (2008). "Neurobiology of Spirituality." *Medicine, Mental Health, Science, Religion, and Well-being* (A.R. Singh and S.A. Singh eds.). *MSM* 6, Jan–Dec 2008. https://pubmed.ncbi.nlm.nih.gov/22013351/.

Mozart, Wolfgang Amadeus. "Piano Sonata No. 16 in C Major." https://www.youtube.com/watch?v=qjk-YRuQZDE. Accessed April 24, 2024.

Neuroscience News. (2015, June 19). "Long Term Musical Memory Spared in Alzheimer's Patients." Retrieved July 7, 2020, from https://neurosciencenews.com/musical-memory-alzheimers-2144/.

Nye, Mary J. "Blackett: Physics, War, and Politics in the Twentieth Century." Cambridge: Harvard University Press, 2004.

"Observer Effect (Physics)." (2023, November 27). *Wikipedia.* https://en.wikipedia.org/wiki/Observer_effect_(physics).

Odenwald, Sten. Stanford University. (2014, June 4). "Gravity Probe B Testing Einstein's Universe." Retrieved June 6, 2020, from https://einstein.stanford.edu/content/relativity/q411.html.

Overduin, J. (2007, November 1). "GRAVITY PROBE B Testing Einstein's Universe." Stanford University. Retrieved June 6, 2020, https://einstein.stanford.edu/SPACETIME/spacetime2.html

"Quantum Foam." (2023, September 29). In *Wikipedia.* https://en.wikipedia.org/wiki/Quantum_foam.

RRS-Radiation Research Society. "In Memoriam: Kurt Hofer (1939-2015)." (2019, October 3). Retrieved June 6, 2020, from https://www.radres.org/news/310525/In-Memoriam-Kurt-Hofer-1939-2015.htm.

Smith, H. (2014, June 4). "What Is a Black *Hole?" NASA Science Space Place*. Retrieved June 6, 2020, from https://www.nasa.gov/audience/forstudents/5-8/features/nasa-knows/what-is-a-black-hole-58.html.

Souders, Beata. "Flow at Work: How to Boost Engagement in the Workplace." *Positive Psychology*, 11 Feb. 2019, https://positivepsychology.com/flow-at-work/. Accessed 7 Jul. 2023.

"Stanley, William Jr." (2023, June 20). *Wikipedia*. https://en.wikipedia.org/wiki/William_Stanley_Jr.

"Statcoulomb." (2023, October 16). *Wikipedia*. https://en.wikipedia.org/wiki/Statcoulomb.

Stein, Rob. "These Scientists Explain the Power of Music to Spark Awe." *npr.org*. (29 Jul. 2023.) www.npr.org/sections/health-shots/2023/07/29/1190374074/these-scientists-explain-the-power-of-music-to-spark-awe#:~:text=%22But%20it%27s%20literally%20true%20—%20your,we%20start%20to%20dance%20together. Accessed 11 Nov. 2023.

The Beverly Hillbillies. Broadcast on CBS from 1962 to 1971. Cast featuring Buddy Ebsen, Irene Ryan, Donna Douglas, and Max Baer Jr. *Wikipedia*. https://en.wikipedia.org/wiki/The_BeverlyHillbillies. Accessed September 12, 2023

The Sound of Music. 1965. Produced and directed by Robert Wise, from a screenplay by Ernest Lehman. Cast: Julie Andrews and Christopher Plummer, with Richard Haydn, Peggy Wood, Charmian Carr, and Eleanor Parker. An adaptation of the 1959 stage musical composed by Richard Rodgers, with lyrics by Oscar Hammerstein

II and a book by Howard Lindsay and Russel Crouse. *Wikipedia*. https://en.wikipedia.org/wiki/The_Sound_of_Music. Accessed August 24, 2023

"Turbulence." *Wikipedia*. https://en.wikipedia.org/wiki/Turbulence. Accessed October 29, 2023.

"Uncertainty Principle." (2023, November 4). *Wikipedia*. https://en.wikipedia.org/wiki/Uncertainty_principle.

University of Utah Health Sciences. (2016, November 29). "This is your brain on God: Spiritual experiences activate brain reward circuits." *ScienceDaily*. Retrieved November 11, 2023 from www.sciencedaily.com/releases/2016/11/161129085014.htm.

van Beethoven, Ludwig. Für Elise. https://www.youtube.com/watch?v=q9bU12gXUyM. Accessed April 23, 2024.

Weisstein, E. W. (n.d.). "Logarithmic Spiral." *Wolfram MathWorld*. Retrieved June 6, 2020, from https://mathworld.wolfram.com/LogarithmicSpiral.html.